Your Soul
at Work

BRUCE HIEBERT

Your Soul
AT Work

How to Live
Your Values in
the Workplace

Northstone

Editor: Michael Schwartzentruber
Cover and interior design: Margaret Kyle
Proofreading: Dianne Greenslade
Cover artwork: www.photos.com

Northstone Publishing is an imprint of Wood Lake Books, Inc. Wood Lake Books acknowledges the financial support of the Government of Canada, through the Book Publishing Industry Development Program (BPIDP) for its publishing activities.

Wood Lake Books is an employee-owned company, committed to caring for the environment and all creation. Wood Lake Books recycles, reuses, and encourages readers to do the same. Resources are printed on recycled paper and more environmentally friendly groundwood papers (newsprint), whenever possible. The trees used are replaced through donations to the Scoutrees For Canada Program. A percentage of all profit is donated to charitable organizations.

Library and Archives Canada Cataloguing in Publication
Hiebert, Bruce, 1957-
Your soul at work : how to live your values in the workplace / Bruce Hiebert.
Previous ed. titled: Good work.
Includes bibliographical references.
ISBN 1-896836-72-0
1. Work--Psychological aspects. 2. Self-actualization (Psychology) 3. Conduct of life.
I. Title.
HD4905.H53 2005   158.7   C2005-900265-4

Published by Northstone Publishing
an imprint of WOOD LAKE BOOKS, INC.
9025 Jim Bailey Road, Kelowna, BC, Canada, V4V 1R2
250.766.2778
www.northstone.com

Printing 10 9 8 7 6 5 4 3 2 1
Printed in Canada by
Transcontinental

Contents

Acknowledgments

As with the previous *Good Work,* this book owes its existence to many communities. I must repeat my thanks to the many folk at Mennonite Central Committee who contributed to and supported me during my initial research into the meaning of work. My thanks also go to the folk I met through Workplace Ministries in Vancouver, British Columbia, and who shared openly their work and their dreams for work. Again special mention goes to Dave Hubert, Jack Klassen, Waldo Neufeld, and Harlene Walker.

I also need to thank my many students at the University of Phoenix, Vancouver campus, who engaged so responsively with the material and who helped me to see its strengths and weaknesses. Greg Nichvalodoff and Angelica Vance made very helpful suggestions. Scott Mitchell's comments in particular led me to a significant rethinking of my basic approach.

Mike Schwartzentruber at Northstone once again did an outstanding job turning my words into well written and coherent prose.

Finally, thanks to Katherine and Gregory, and most especially to Marlene, for the support that makes this possible.

1

Life Is Work

The Nature of the Journey

Life is work.

It is such a simple statement, but it masks such incredible profundity and complexity. Yes, life is work: most of our adult waking hours will be spent in some form of "work" activity. And at the same time, we work at our lives, engaging in a constant effort to transform ourselves into the best that we can be. At another level, our identity is caught up in the "work" that we do. We say, "I am_____" and fill in the blank with some current work title. Even as we end our days of paid employment, we say, "I am a retired _____."

One of my former staff helped me to see this clearly. He was a master gardener, a professional horticulturalist. A local firm had hired him from overseas. Then, less than a year later, they fired him. His family depended on him; his citizenship depended on his work. He had no one to turn to, no family to help out, nothing. He

We are intrinsically part of all that is, and since work is one of our major forms of engagement with all that is, work is one of the most fundamental activities of life – and the primal enactment of its essence.

was devastated. Someone recommended he come to me for advice and he did so. I immediately saw his ability and value to a project I was running at the time.

The next three months were very difficult for him. He did well at the work, despite a steep learning curve. But what made the sweat bead on his brow was the work he had to do with his identity. In order to do what I needed done, he had to rethink his whole existence; he had never had a desk job before and from his point of view that was not who he "was." So he worked at it, often coming to work in purest agony. But he did it; he changed his sense of his identity to match his new work. Then, three months later, he applied for and was given a job with a horticultural supply company, a job that brought together both his old and his new work identities. He loved the new job. But as he said to me later, he could never have applied for the job if I had not forced him to rework his existence.

Yet even this depth of "inter-wovenness" between our individual existence and "work" misses something that is much deeper, and much more profound. Our lives are part of the cosmos itself. Every breath we take is the breathing of the universe; every thought we make is the thinking of creation itself; every act of work we undertake is the outworking of existence itself. We are intrinsically part of all that is, and since work is one of our major forms of engagement with all that is, work is one of the most fundamental activities of life – and the primal enactment of its essence.

We can think of our work this way. Each day when we arise, we begin to fabricate our existence; we begin to fabricate our way of engaging those around us. Then we go into the world to work: to rear children, operate a business, teach, manage, construct, or do whatever our talents, experience, and skills lead us to. Finally, we place all of that into the context of what we wish to achieve with our lives, reflecting (sometimes) at the end of the day on who we are and what we have done.

At the same time, that progression from waking to sleeping, with work between, represents a movement in the transformation of the universe itself, a transformation from what *was* to what *will be*. At the end of each day, the universe is different than it was at the beginning, and our work is one of the most important aspects of that change.

It is that range of meaning that this book engages. Starting with our understanding of work itself, this book progressively follows each step of the day, moving from how we think about how to engage the world to how we actually complete the work we take on. Think of this book as a meditation on the nature of our work, on our constructive engagement with the universe itself, and on our enactment of the very meaning of existence.

Each of us will spend more of our waking hours working, or preparing for work, or recovering from work, than we will spend on any other activity in our whole lives.

Fundamental to this book is the realization that each of us will spend more of our waking hours working, or preparing for work, or recovering from work, than we will spend on any other activity in our whole lives. Yet our training, background, and the contemporary world leave us unprepared for this and vulnerable to every shift of our economy, technology, and environment. If we are to make full and good use of our lives, we must *know* better and *do* better when it comes to our work. Our work needs to reflect our understanding of the meaning of our lives and engage the universe at the level of its best construction.

This book comes out of my own journey into the meaning of work. I am in my mid-40s and have, for the second time in my life, found a deeply satisfying place to work, one where I can feel the ripples of my work moving from my soul into the universe itself. I have spent time in many companies and organizations, as an employee, manager, owner, and consultant. Each position has taught me something new about people, work, and the meaning of work. Some of that work has been extraordinarily frustrating, and some of it has left me profoundly moved, sometimes by my own work and sometimes by the example and efforts of those around me. Currently, I derive deep pleasure from the teaching and consulting work that I do. I know that my work reflects what I believe to be ultimately true and, when I work to the best of my abilities, carries the universe into a better future.

Almost ten years ago, I reflected on the nature of work in my book *Good Work*. This new book bears many similarities to that earlier reflection and careful readers will notice many places of overlap and even a few shared words. But I find that in the ten years since I wrote *Good Work*, my views have changed at many levels and that much of what I wrote then no longer seems relevant now. Colleagues, co-workers, and students have all contributed to these new understandings. I believe that I see the world, and the connections between work and the meaning of existence, with far greater clarity than I did then. I believe that this is, therefore, a new work on my part. Perhaps, in another ten years, my journey will bring me back once again, with new understanding and even more clarity. One thing I do know; having begun to think intensely and deeply about work, I am unable to cease reflecting on that part of my journey. I only hope I can contribute something that will assist you in your own journey.

Spirituality

For the rest of this book to make sense, I need to explain the view of life and the universe that underlies it.

I believe in God. I don't know if my God is the God of traditional Christian orthodoxy – that call I leave to someone else – but I am convinced that the universe we live in is designed for us. Not just for us humans, but for all life, and for growth and change and beauty. I also believe the universe is suffused by One who works with us, enhancing our experience, sharing in our joys, weeping with our sorrows, and carefully enticing us into a world of deeper communion with each other and with existence itself.

We are not here by accident, and while we have not been given an outline of what we are to do (if we had been, this book would be unnecessary) we can know, from time to time and in specific places, that what we are doing is "Right."

This perspective leaves me with the conviction that everything I see and everything I do finds its ultimate meaning in something much greater than myself. My actions may ultimately mean and may ultimately lead to things – either good or bad – I never consciously meant or intended. Forces of good (and sometimes of evil) sneak out of the cracks of existence and into our lives, transforming us, sometimes when we are less than completely aware, and assisting (or inhibiting) us as we strive to accomplish our purpose in life. The world around us is not only human and material, but also divine and spiritual.

I believe that each of us has a purpose in life – sometimes many purposes. We are not here by accident, and while we have not been given an outline of what we are to do (if we had been, this book would be unnecessary) we can know, from time to time and in specific places, that what we are doing is "Right." I mean Right in the cosmic sense: the thing the universe calls forth from us; the one thing we can bring to that moment to make the universe what it needs to be. Some people find that Right in their job. Some find it in the very shape of their existence. And some find it in the moment, in the confluence of events, people, and place. For some of us, that Right leaves us burned out, consumed by the universe for the good that was needed. For others, that Right warms and energizes them into an enduring graciousness towards whatever life brings. Some of us wander a long time, looking for that confluence and feeling that tells us we have done Right. And for some, life brings all of the above.

I certainly believe that my life has a purpose. Sometimes I have carried it out; sometimes I have occupied myself with other things; and sometimes I have felt I was being prepared for some new Right. This purpose is not, for most of us, a static thing. But it is real and it is waiting for us (again).

This means that our lives work at many levels. Day to day, we carry out those mundane tasks, those seemingly meaningless routines that fill our lives. At another level, though, those same tasks and routines help us to carry out our purpose and the intentions we have for our lives. As we travel deeper, we discover the level of our values, convictions, and deepest aspirations. And finally, deeper still, we discover how these engage us in the underlying nature of existence, in its movement toward greater beauty.

These levels are not always in harmony, and when they are not, we feel the discord. Because there is purpose, we know when things are coming together and when they are coming apart. So these levels have their own shifting relationship.

The society within which we work adds a further complication. Society is a work in progress, the collective movement of humanity toward its place in the cosmos, and a place in which each of us must make our way. As my students have pointed out to me, what we can accomplish, what we can realize of our personal purpose, depends to some degree on how our society is accomplishing *its* purpose. If our society is not moving appropriately, then it becomes increasingly difficult for people, as individuals, to move appropriately. We must move together, or it becomes increasingly difficult to move at all. We exist within a social web; that exists within a planetary, ecological web; that exists within a cosmic web of meaning. Our lives, which are always undergoing transformation at a personal level, are also part of a greater transformation, of which we are only one small part, a transformation in which society and the cosmos itself dance with us, pushing us and pulling us, this way and that.

We exist within a social web; that exists within a planetary, ecological web; that exists within a cosmic web of meaning.

Paradoxically, this profound level of interaction between our work, the work of society, and the work of the cosmos makes our individual lives more important, not less. If the work of our lives is part of the work of society and the work of the cosmos, and our work is assisted or inhibited by society and cosmos, then we find ourselves, potentially, at each moment, on the cusp of action which could change everything. When we act, it could be the door that opens (or closes) an opportunity for society and the cosmos. We may be acting to enable everything to flow to its correct place, or we may be interfering with that flow, imprisoning not only ourselves, but those around us, and the universe itself. So while we may feel powerless against society and lost in the cosmos, the complex reality is that each moment and each action counts. We never know when our small part is the one that will be needed by all.

Historically, none of this has been very relevant to most people. At most times and in places, people's daily activities have been proscribed by their circumstances: their family, their community, their inherited occupation, their economic needs, and so on. Very few people had the opportunity to explore the integration of day-to-day existence with the fundamental forces of the universe. The search for meaning on that level took place primarily in sacred assemblies and through special rites, perhaps in a church or temple or synagogue. Much more rarely, it might have happened around the dinner table or among friends. But it was not something most people paid attention to in the same way we are able to do today.

Today we experience more wealth and personal prosperity than at any time in history. Many poor live with better health and greater freedom than did kings of old. In addition, today there are at least 20,000 occupational categories in North America, with more being added all the time. We are not boxed in by our circumstances. We don't even climb a career ladder any longer so much as we embark upon a personal career journey. Today we make our way following aptitude, circumstance, and interest. We can take our work into our own hands. We can choose how we earn our daily bread.

The opportunity to choose and the huge variety of choices available to us make all the difference in the world. Now, however, we face the growing awareness that with our choices come responsibilities. We must make decisions, but do we have the tools to make those decisions well? The ability to make wise decisions requires awareness, training, and experience. This book tries to meet that need. We can think about our work in new ways: ways that reflect the Right, that fulfill our purpose, and that bring us into harmony with the One who made, maintains, and improves all things.

Struggle

Work is not easy. That's why we call it "work"!

We "work" at our lives; we expend effort and energy; we are weighed down; we struggle. While I am convinced that work represents our most important engagement with the ultimates of existence, it is often work itself that most interferes with this. Rare is the person who goes to work empty and comes home full of energy. For most of us, the tasks of the day leave us with less than we started. At work, we sometimes face overwhelming responsibility, pointless tasks, futile efforts, and painstaking repetition. Even the routine, comforting as it can be, takes energy out of us. The problem is how to take on the responsibility our very existence brings when we are too caught up in just getting the work done. We know we "should" do more, but where do we find the time and energy?

We must connect deeply and purposefully with our center, with that which surrounds and sustains us, and which drives the universe itself.

Paradoxically, we can also experience resistance to the realization of the possibilities in our work and the need for new approaches to it. We construct our lives slowly, out of many decisions, many actions, both thoughtful and accidental. Over time, our lives become encrusted with a buildup of habit and routine, both our own and those of the people around us. Our community, friends, co-workers, spouses, partners, and children come to understand us in specific ways and to support our long-term patterns, no matter how much we might come to see the need for change. Because we are connected in this web of relationships, *our* patterns are *their* patterns, and *our* change *is*, like it or not, *their* change. This dynamic can make change much harder.

While I believe that our work can liberate the fundamental forces of the universe to Good and be highly energizing to us, the levels of our existence don't all run the same way at the same time. If we are to proceed, we will need the help of others and the ability to rely on those powers that sustain us.

My hope is that this book will help you to *see* better and therefore to *act* better; and even more, to *be* better. To me, this means we must connect deeply and purposefully with our center, with that which surrounds and sustains us, and which drives the universe itself. This means giving up control over our own lives in some very scary ways. We must trust that the One who so lovingly crafted the universe will work with us, if we open ourselves and allow ourselves to be vulnerable, if we expose our partialness, our weakness, and our hurt. If we are ever to find our purpose, we must volunteer our lives to the One.

If we embrace the challenge, surrender to the One, and keep putting one foot in front of the other, we will find ourselves merging into the One with all the joy that fills the universe.

Joy

Having said those things, I want to emphasize one last point – persevering through the first steps is the most liberating thing we can do. If we embrace the challenge, surrender to the One, and keep putting one foot in front of the other, we will find ourselves merging into the One with all the joy that fills the universe. Our small steps will be matched and multiplied. Every step we take opens doorways, cracks into the core of the cosmos that make the struggle worth it.

I know in my own life that this struggle can be overwhelming. I've lost it, from time to time. I have gone the wrong way out of exhaustion, loss of spirit, and personal or financial setbacks. At those times, even the positive steps we may have taken previously seem to lose their brightness and their meaning. But I also know from experience that even stepping off the road can be a way to stepping back on the road, transformed and reinvigorated. And then it happens. There is a flash of joy so wonderful that you realize all the work has been worthwhile. In that moment, you know that you have done well.

Put simply, work is really all about joy.

2

Being
Work & Identity

Work is central to identity.

Granted, that is not the way we typically like to think about our work. Usually, we like to keep our core identity and our work separate. But in many key respects, we cannot do so, even if we think we have them compartmentalized.

The most obvious place to see this is in relation to job loss. In my case, it was utterly clear how much I identified my "job" with my "identity" when I was fired from my work as a church minister. When it happened, I stepped almost instantaneously out of a job, out of a role with which I identified very strongly, and into an abyss. It was a time of heavy denial for me, though not of my job loss, which I accepted with some relief since it had become a very difficult job for reasons beyond my control, but of the effect of this change on my identity. For at least six months, part of me continued to act as if I still had my old job.

It was a time of heavy denial for me, though not of my job loss, which I accepted with some relief since it had become a very difficult job for reasons beyond my control, but of the effect of this change on my identity.

I behaved in keeping with its norms. I talked to others with the language and as if I had the responsibility that went with my old job. Eventually, to my utter humiliation, friends started commenting on my refusal to step out of the role, though in fact – and this was the real source of the humiliation – I had not realized until then that I was still acting out of it.

From the very first time some-one asks us, as little children, what we want to be when we grow up, we begin to think of ourselves in terms of "our" job.

I know I was not unique in this behavior. I have heard of laid-off bankers who continue for months to get dressed in suit and tie, pick up the briefcase, and head downtown, even if only to spend the day at the library. I did nothing that extreme (at least from my point of view!), but I know it took a long time for my sense of "identity" to catch up with the reality of my unemployment.

We are mind-body unities. Everything we do and think shapes everything *else* we do and *think* we are. When we take on a job, we "become" that job, at least in part. When we leave a job, we still carry that job inside us, and it changes the way we think about ourselves and relate to those around us.

Why this happens is not hard to see. From the very first time someone asks us, as little children, what we want to be when we grow up, we begin to think of ourselves in terms of "our" job. Later, we go through schooling and learning designed to ready us for work. By the time we actually enter the working world, the tendency to identify ourselves with our work is thoroughly engrained. "What do you do?" is the question that most frequently follows "What is your name?" Sometimes it's the *first* question.

Identity is a funny thing for most of us. We name ourselves as businessmen, teachers, lawyers, nurses, housewives, gar-bage collectors, doctors, and writers with an ease completely out of keeping with the complexity of what we are doing in that naming. Each of these "titles" addresses us not "as we really are," but through our role in the workplace. For those who work with us, the job site may be their only point of contact with us. For them, "who we really are" is often "who we are on the job." We may complain about this (and rightly so sometimes) but should we begin to step outside that role in inappropriate ways, such as when a boss sees him/herself as a potential lover, all sorts of bad things can happen.

Yet this role identity continues even off the job. Our families, though they do not relate to us on the job (or did not until the recent surge in home-based businesses), are also not immune from identifying us with our work. Likewise, our broader community of friends and acquaintances very often make assumptions about our probable likes and dislikes, intelligence, creativity, lifestyle, social standing, etc., based on the labels we use to describe our work.

For most of us, all of this simply feeds our own sense of identity and worth. Some of us fight it, and some of us succeed in breaking out of the molds our work may cast us in, but all of us are affected by our workplace identity.

Yet we are not only mind-body unities, we are also an integral part of the web of all life on the planet. Our work, our identity, our community, our well-being, our social existence, and our planet, are all interrelated. We cannot change or engage in one without changing all the others. Who we "are" is found in what we do, and what we do transforms us and the world around us so that everything reflects what we have done.

This concerns me because the spiritual journey we make when we attempt to find and do soul work is not one we can hold separate from who we are and what we experience in the workplace. For example, if my work leads to a sense of worthlessness, my spiritual journey becomes dark and empty.

(This is one of the central problems caused by unemployment. Idled workers feel worthless and withdraw into themselves.) On the other hand, if I am lucky enough to experience work as an outlet for my creativity, this can have an extremely energizing effect on my spirituality.

But my deeper concern in all this is that the labels we use to define ourselves as workers are simply too superficial. We need to move beyond the common labels, which serve mostly to identify professional categories or tasks. (We are doctors, lawyers, teachers, welders, etc.) Our identity in the workplace *is* important, but the central or most important feature of that identity is *not* the specific job we do.

I believe there are *five* archetypal roles we embody and that come alive for us in our work, regardless of the type of work we do. Some of these roles are ancient, some are more recent "inventions," but *all* of them are crucial as part of our self-definition as workers. It is *these* roles and their relationship to good work that we must understand. In fact, I believe that good work springs directly from one of these roles in particular. But I am jumping ahead of myself. Let us take these roles in turn.

Provider

The oldest and most basic role we play as workers is that of *provider*. The provider is the one who brings the resources necessary for group survival. This role stretches back to our very earliest forebears and can be found among many animals. The parents of many species provide food and shelter for their offspring through their efforts and skill. Among us moderns, this type of behavior is called "earning a living." The role of provider is a highly egalitarian one: both men and women, old and young, can assist with providing the resources needed for survival as a family or group.

The provider role is viewed and experienced very positively by ourselves and those around us. All communities need providers in order to survive and prosper. Those who provide usually receive positive feedback from the group because their efforts help to make the group healthier and happier. And as a result of this feedback, those who provide usually experience pride and esteem knowing they have done well for the community.

I believe there are five arche-typal roles we embody and that come alive for us in our work, regardless of the type of work we do.

Spiritually, the provider role reminds us of our fundamental physicality. No journey is possible if we do not have the physical resources to make it. No life is possible if we do not have the physical resources to live it. As providers, we also learn to recognize and work with one of the fundamental laws of the universe – all things must participate in the cycles of birth, growth, and death. Providers must face the universal truth that the cost of our sustenance usually includes the death of other living things. As providers, we are involved in the ultimate drama of life itself.

Unfortunately, the value of this archetype has become obscured by the complexity and insensitivity of our culture. Though we may seek to be providers, it is difficult, in our technological culture, to raise this role and to celebrate it independent of our modern role of *consumers*. Too often, we celebrate the provision of resources, not as something achieved in partnership with nature, but as an example of our power *over* nature and as a prelude to gluttonous, destructive consumption. When we over-consume, we provide with the sense not that we have met our family's vital needs, but that we have staved off the predators, the bill collectors, the credit agencies – those who stand between us and the real providers of the "necessities" we subscribe to.

The simple dignity of providing has been mostly lost and with it we have lost its spirituality. Regardless, the role is still important, and provides one of the basic building blocks of our identity and spirituality. We would do well to remember and celebrate this role.

Bringer of Wealth

The *bringer of wealth* is closely related to the *provider,* but there are differences in how the two roles are perceived and therefore how they are treated in society.

Wealth is what you have when you have more than enough, or when you *sense* that you have more than enough. Wealth is about feeling secure and perceiving plenty. If you think of wealth in terms of creature comforts, then you can easily see that most of us have far more in the way of wealth than did the kings of history. But that does not mean we *feel* wealthy. What we want is to feel secure *today*, with a surplus for *tomorrow*. This is a psychological state based on many things, not just on what we have provided. Therefore, the bringer of wealth is the one who satisfies those feelings and perceptions. For most of us, that looks like big savings accounts, fine homes, lots of travel, good restaurants, private schools, and fancy cars. It also looks like stable economies, strong borders, and good pensions. In fact, when we look around, we can see that most of what we are about in our society is "bringing wealth." This is very often the main product of what we do!

The value of this role is ambiguous; it is not necessarily a good thing for either the individual or society. To really grapple with this, we need to look back into pre-history. For our hunting and gathering ancestors, wealth looked a lot like meat. When the hunters brought home a big animal (or more than one), the tribe knew they had more than enough. So far so good. But now, facing a surplus, the tribe needed to bring into play social mechanisms for deciding who would get how much – who would get the extra portion, or the best portion. Should it go to the elders (former hunters who regulated the hunt), or to the best hunters (those who made the wealth possible)? Such communities (or their most powerful members) generally agreed that it should *not* go to the women or the children. The weak would receive what was left over. *They* were not bringers of wealth, no matter how many of the basics of life they may have provided (and, in gathering and hunting societies, women gathered most of the needs of daily life). Wealth was a function of the hunt, which happened away from hearth and home. Wealth, therefore, belonged to those who went out and got it.

Once we start exchanging respect for wealth, we begin to create destructive divisions within society.

You can see the problem. Wealth becomes part of a structure of power. Those who bring home wealth are given status. Status is what the rest of us offer in return for getting our hands on some of the "meat." But once we start exchanging *respect* for *wealth*, we begin to create destructive divisions within society.

The first division is between those who bring wealth and those who depend on it, but who do not directly create it. The first group is viewed positively (everyone looks up to those who bring wealth) and the second negatively (someone else did the work, and *you* should be grateful). Due to the realities of pregnancy and childcare, women have traditionally fallen into the second group.

The second division is between the bringers of wealth themselves. This is the fundamental distinction between those who are "successful" and those who are not.

The consequences of these two divisions are tremendous. As we have seen, what has been traditionally thought of as "women's work" loses its value in the eyes of both men and women. Regardless of the vital role women play in the maintenance of the group, the *wealth* belongs to someone else and so, therefore, does the esteem. Women become second-class citizens. As a result, their desires, hopes, dreams, and spiritual aspirations also take second place to those of men. Only in the last century, with the growth of feminism and the increasing numbers of women entering the industrial, business, and service workforces has this begun to change.

While historically the first division has not treated women kindly, the consequence of the second division (between those who are "successful" at bringing wealth and those who are not) has been no picnic for men. What happens to the man who cannot provide wealth? "Worse than a woman" is not an insult anyone is likely to mutter today, but it certainly was in the past. The hunter who could not provide wealth in days gone by, and the man who cannot provide wealth today, experiences this lack or inability at the core of his being. It is the source of much spiritual anguish.

In fact, there is only one "winner" in this whole scenario – the person who brings wealth. For that reason, I believe it is virtually impossible to do truly good work, our soul work, if this is the only role we embody. Bringing wealth is a good thing, but it is, most definitely, not the *only* thing.

Person of Excellence

"Excellence" is something our species has always strived for. At whatever skill we have needed, we have worked hard to become the best we can be. And among us there have always been those who have achieved a level of excellence we call "mastery."

This pursuit and its accomplishment give rise to one of the most powerful emotional and spiritual roles our work can give us. In accomplishing excellence, we experience a feeling of personal satisfaction. At one time, the well-shot bow, the straight furrow, the tidy knit and weave, and the sculpted lines of the pot left us feeling good about ourselves. And, in the admiration of others who had also tried (and sometimes mastered) these skills, there was yet more good feeling. Accomplishment, social respect, personal power: all these radiated from "mastery."

What's important to notice, however, is not so much the technical skill but the change in being that results from mastery. Being good *at* something makes us feel *worthy*. We become different persons: more confidant, capable, powerful; more in harmony by virtue of our accomplishment.

In accomplishing excellence, we experience a feeling of personal satisfaction.

In our world, the role of *person of excellence* has been primarily captured by the *professional*. While as a culture we are still sensitive to the mastery of crafts, technical skills, and various artistic and athletic pursuits, we typically reserve our greatest respect and pride for "professionals."

The role of professional derives from two things: excellence with a set of skills, and recognition by a regulatory body. At one time, the regulators were guilds. Now they are professional societies or associations, or doctor's or teacher's colleges. Once you have mastered the skills deemed necessary by the regulatory body, and have been accepted into their company, you are a *professional*. Much like the craft masters of the past, the professional bears within him or herself a particular role in our community, a role which comes from both the type and manner of working.

In our society, professional status entitles one to esteem and respect – esteem and respect by virtue of the role itself, and regardless of the person. This is a curious phenomenon, and, like many things about work, it is a two-edged sword. On the face of it, it is remarkable that we would value a person not on the basis of their character, but only on the basis of mastery of skills and recognition by a professional body. Yet we do it every day.

On the other hand, the role reflects a reality: mastery needs recognition if we as a community are to live together. We need to identify those who can be trusted for their competence. We need to be able to identify whom to call upon for assistance, advice, and training. This is a profoundly important function in a complex society. We do not know each other personally. When we need important services such as medicine, law, or education, we cannot simply go to the phone book white pages, pick a name, and assume that this or that person will be able to provide the necessary assistance. Page after page of names rolls by and we have no idea who is the right person to contact to evaluate our illness, advise us on our mortgage, or teach our children. We have to look for those who are recognized, legitimate, and qualified, and we do so by requiring professional certification. In this way, we know that even though we personally do not know the where's and what's of their training, the mere fact that they have the license or accreditation means that they are probably good for us.

There is yet another side effect of this role. When we become professionals, we are often changed by that recognition. Because we are trusted, we often become more trustworthy. Because we are esteemed, we often feel better about ourselves. Because we have been tested for competence, we often work hard to maintain that status. As others perceive us as trusted, esteemed, or competent, their perceptions become, for many of us, a standard we try to live up to. This is not universally true, of course, and we can all identify betrayals of professional standards, but that very sense of betrayal indicates how powerfully we expect professionals to behave in specific ways.

Despite the problems that can arise around this role, it is a profound and positive one, which we need in order to work together.

Pilgrim

Another archetypal role we may embody in our work speaks to our potential as "growing persons" or *pilgrims*. Throughout our lives, we are on a journey toward wisdom and peace, and we often forget that it is in the course of our work that we meet many of the challenges through which we mature as individuals. In our work, we confront people, issues, and opportunities that force us to change and grow.

The sense of competence we learn, the graciousness we learn, the emotions we deal with, and the skills we pick up, almost always influence every aspect of our lives, including our inner spiritual journey.

This growth has traditionally been the rationale for granting seniority, and for promotion based on seniority. In the past, our growth as individuals in skill, wisdom, and understanding, resulted in increased job security, higher income, and greater opportunities for promotion. This is not so much the case today, but, even so, we still regard the transformations we undergo through work as positive contributions to our identity.

As we grow in wisdom through our work, we also grow in wisdom through all aspects of our life. Being forced to learn to deal graciously with nasty customers can set us free to deal graciously with life outside the workplace. Being challenged to learn new management methods can allow us to learn new ways to resolve other life issues.

Unfortunately, we often overlook this aspect of work because we tend to separate work from what is important to our inner lives. But the sense of competence we learn, the graciousness we learn, the emotions we deal with, and the skills we pick up, almost always influence every aspect of our lives, including our inner spiritual journey. We will return to this at a later point, because it is through this role that we come to recognize in our work not just a personal context, but a spiritual journey.

Entrepreneur-Artist

The fifth role, and the one on which I want to spend the most time, is the archetypal role of *entrepreneur* or *artist*. While this may seem to be a strange, even contradictory, set of labels, nonetheless, it describes a vitally important part of the way each of us lives from day to day. Even more, it is from this role that the essential nature of soul work springs.

Until we act to transform, the future exists as a vast range of possibilities.

I use the term *entrepreneur-artist* to acknowledge the reality that *in* and *through* our work, the world is transformed from one thing to another by design. Every day, each of us takes what we have, imagines new possibilities and makes decisions about the most effective way to bring those possibilities to reality. Then, rather than crawl back under the covers, we step forward and take the risk of acting to change the world on that basis.

While we do not readily think of it this way, our work is a *risky venture* that *creates* the future. Work is not random scattered activity, but instead is driven by human imagination and risk taking. Human work is the interface between *what is* and *what could be*, and it always leads to what *will be*. Based only on our imagination, we risk what is in order to create what will be.

This ability is no small thing. Our ability to transform is what gives us hope and joy. It is what creates the sense of satisfaction we feel in our work. Our ability to transform reaches *in*, to the core of our being, to our inmost drives and images; and *out* to the farthest reaches of our space-time and culture. It is as risk takers and creators that we reach the pinnacle of what it means to be human and faithful. Transformation of our world, through imagination and risk, is the essence of our journey.

Our ability to creatively transform the world is expressed in everything we do, whether we are a machinist who takes a bar of steel and turns it into a piece of equipment, or a manager who works to mold people and processes, or an environmentalist who seeks to save our natural environment, or a social activist who lobbies government for more just and equitable distribution of wealth in society. For this reason, it is a power we must consider carefully.

Until we act to transform, the future exists as a vast range of possibilities. Think of a corridor full of doors, each waiting to be opened. Behind each door is a possibility that may be brought into or excluded from existence. When we act, we are opening one of those doors, bringing that option into existence. And once a new option exists, all the others are excluded, at least for that moment. Having made the choice, we have created a new world.

In my case, whether I write this word or that word changes what you read, and (maybe) what you think, and (hopefully) what you do. But having written the word, I cannot easily un-make that choice (once it is printed). The impact it has (may have) is set in motion. My words are already out there and I cannot change how you respond. My work has created my (and possibly your) future.

That also is the risk. Having made the choice to act, we can never fully know what will happen. Once I have created something, it becomes virtually impossible to un-create it – to put the genie back into the bottle. You will read what I have written, and not something else I *could* have written, and, for good or ill, you will be affected. If I later discover that I have erred, I can only hope that the error has no great consequence. Or I must try to further transform that error into something better – which demands even more work and involves further risk of misstep.

This, perhaps as much as anything, reveals the shadow side of our work. Our errors, limitations, and problems have created a world that is less than it could be. Of all possible worlds, ours is not the best, and in some respects that is our fault. It was not the best when we inherited it and our limitations as creators ensure that it will be even less than it could have been when we die. Our actions have consequences and they are never all positive. Even worse, sometimes, we are seriously wrong. We, as creators of the future, are always open to the risk of serious error.

Transformation is the key to soul work. It is in our role as creators and risk takers that we do soul work.

Yet there is also potential in our limitations and in this situation we inherit. Although things are less than the best, we have been given the possibility of improving the world. Furthermore, just as we cannot know all the negative consequences of our work, neither can we know the full positive scope of our actions. While we never create "the best," we can improve upon what we are given (sometimes accidentally). When this type of transformation takes place it often represents our very best work.

There is another risk inherent in this role. It is far too easy for our ability to create to go to our heads. Just because we *can* create something does not mean we *should* create it. Forgetting that moral caution (this is a caution, not an imperative. An imperative says you "must" do something), we have let loose on the planet unimaginable destruction. We have only to remember the death camps or the atom bomb to recognize the danger our creative risk taking can produce. At a more personal level, it is not good for any one of us to get carried away with the knowledge of our power to create the future. We can become arrogant and dangerous in small ways as well as large.

Still, this is not to deny the positive power of our role as creators. Our human potential to do good is tremendous. Even our *failures* are often magnificent, and sometimes, in kind of a cosmic ironic twist, *better* for being failures. It is as if there is a grace that gets into this world through our failures and uses them as a beginning point for something better.

Transformation is the key to soul work. It is in our role as creators and risk takers that we *do* soul work. But before we explore the nature of soul work itself, there is one other issue we must grapple with first, and that is the economy.

The Economy

Since our work is so profoundly intertwined with our sense of identity, it should come as no surprise that the economy, the vast engine within which we work, plays a role here, too. The economic realities we encounter when we first enter the work force influence greatly, for good or ill, our experience of who we are in relation to our work. For example, the person who has to wait in line with hundreds of other applicants for one job opening will see the world and come to view him or herself very differently than the person who found a job simply by asking at the place with the sign in the window. If these experiences occur repeatedly, the differences in experience will lead to profoundly different beliefs about how the world of work *actually* operates, how we as workers *must* behave, and maybe even in who we *really* are.

Economic cycles are key to all of this. In other words, we will see and experience the workplace and ourselves in relation to it in a very different way from previous or succeeding generations, depending on when in the economic cycle we were born. Each generation enters the workforce and feels its own experience to be *true*, failing to understand that the massive changes in the economy over time mean that what we experience is only *true for us*, and that colleagues working beside us may, because they entered the workforce at a different point in the economic cycle, see the world quite differently than we do.

To return to the example above, easy access to a job – the experience of many who were born in the 1940s and the 1980s – will likely lead to a positive evaluation of the working world's opportunities and will provide a sense of competence in managing a career. For those at the leading edge of the baby boom in particular, especially men, the economy was strong and the world of work was a good place, where obedience and showing up were all that was required for substantial economic success. These people could loyally invest themselves in their work and expect to be rewarded. For them, jobs and self-esteem, good feelings and a sense of competence flowed out of their workplace experience. They did not need to ask themselves what "soul work" meant, because almost any work was soul work.

By comparison, having to wait in line with increasingly qualified workers – the experience of those born between the late 1950s and the mid-1970s – will likely lead to a sense of intense competition and frustration with the workplace. For the people born between the 1950s and 1970s, loyalty was very often *not* rewarded. Simply showing up was no guarantee of anything. Opportunity only came to those with good luck, outstanding ability, or good connections. As new technology and ways of working were introduced, no one knew which types of work would prosper and which would not. Even those who prospered never knew if next week they would be out of work. In fact, under some circumstances, prosperity and good luck would themselves lead to unemployment as a result of competitive pressures or corporate buy-outs.

It is within the context of these latter circumstances that soul work becomes an especially important idea. For workers facing turmoil, regular job loss, and a bizarre expanse of possibilities, discovering what soul work is, and then finding it and making it a part of your life, becomes tremendously significant. (In this, they are joined by those of every generation who have sought to make sense out of their lives and work, and to live lives of meaning beyond mere financial success.)

Of course, these are gross generalizations and do not apply to everyone. Across North America, there have been times of prosperity and experiences of hardship quite outside the overall economic experience. And many workers come from other cultures, with very different work experiences.

More importantly, beyond all those considerations lies the larger truth that no matter how important they seem, we are ultimately not our jobs and not our roles; we are travelers on a journey, pilgrims seeking a home. Doing good work, soul work, is one of the most important parts of that journey. And so it is to understanding what makes for such work that we turn next.

For workers facing turmoil, regular job loss, and a bizarre expanse of possibilities, discovering what soul work is, and then finding it and making it a part of your life, becomes tremendously significant.

3

Soul Work

The Nature of Work

If you are reading this book, it is probably because you want to do "soul work." You are looking for that creative engagement that *challenges* you and at the same *expresses* what is most important to you.

An acquaintance, a local manager in an enormous government bureaucracy, once confided to me that he saw his work as a reflection of his spiritual beliefs and commitments. He was convinced that what he was doing was improving the world. I was a little taken aback by the confession, in part because of my long-standing suspicion of bureaucrats. But, as I thought about it, I realized he was correct. While the larger bureaucracy of which he was a part was not particularly noted for its generosity, sensitivity, or compassion, I had to recall that his particular section was noted for just those characteristics. His staff was also remarkable for their high morale,

All work starts with an act of imagination; we envision what it is we want to do. Then we set out with the intention of achieving that goal. Next, using that imaginative picture and our intention to direct us, we apply our skills and efforts to some resource through a process.

long-term commitment to public service, forward thinking, and flexibility. The more I thought about it, the more I came to agree that he had taken his values and created a work situation that nurtured "soul work."

So what exactly is soul work?

There are two aspects to soul work. The first has to do with the nature of work itself. The second has to do with the question of whether the particular work you are engaged in is soul work *for you*. In this chapter, we will look at the first of these two aspects: the nature of work.

When we look closely at work, we see that it actually has a number of components. All work starts with an act of *imagination;* we envision what it is we want to do. Then we set out with the *intention* of achieving that goal. Next, using that *imaginative picture* and our *intention* to direct us, we apply our *skills* and *efforts* to some *resource* through a *process*. A resource can be anything from time; to some material; to a natural resource, such as a tree or some form of energy; to potential customers. As we apply our skills and efforts through a process to this resource, it is transformed into a *product:* perhaps a hard good such as a toaster, or a service. Along the way, we always produce *by-products*, which can be either positive or negative. On the negative side, there is always wasted energy, or unused or unusable materials, for example. On the positive side, the by-product of our work may be satisfied customers, or the satisfaction we feel ourselves knowing we have done our work well. There are also a series of other results, such as *unintended consequences* and *learning*. Every action, especially one as complex as our work, yields unintended consequences, results we do not plan for, do not expect, which nevertheless become inevitable once we have taken our actions. In terms of *learning*, not only does our work change our world, it also changes *us*, through what we learn as we do the work. Finally, all work takes place within a field of *opportunity*. All work takes place in the context of the work and actions of others, work and actions that make our work possible.

If we draw it as a diagram it looks like this:

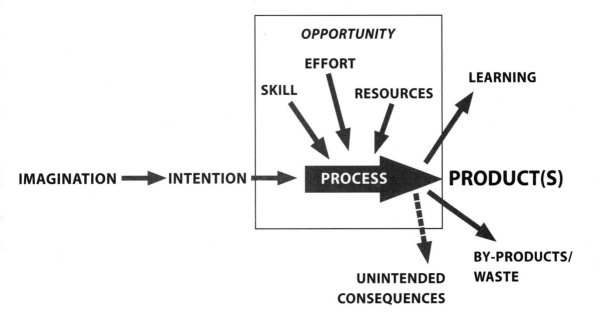

All work involves each of these components. Soul work, in its fullest sense, is work that resonates with our identity at each one of these levels, in both the short-term and long-term. When we find such work – where imagination, intentions, skills, efforts, resources, processes, products, by-products, unintended consequences, and learning are each good, and they work together in a supportive environment – we have indeed found work that will both reflect and actively engage our soul.

Let's look at each of these components in more depth, seeking to discover how we can, as persons of integrity, use each one to more fully embody our deepest energies.

Imagination

All work begins with an act of imagination, even if the task in front of us is routine. We must be able to imagine a possible outcome before we can proceed. We must be able to hold in our heads some sort of imagined consequence of our actions before we can guide our body to perform the necessary work. We must be able to imagine how the resources at our command can be manipulated into the shape and form we need to accomplish our desires.

We use our imagination so often and so naturally, that we tend to lose sight of the magic of what we are doing.

For an architect, this involves the ability to hold a whole building in his or her head, to imagine people living and working within a massive physical structure. Then this imagining must be re-imagined as models and lines on paper, which can be used to guide other people's imaginations. Engineers must take what has been put on paper and be able to imagine what sort of materials, steel locations, reinforcements, conduits, and wiring will be necessary to make the building come alive. Still other workers must be able to imagine how these lines and directions are to take shape as actual forms for concrete, ducting for heat, and wiring for electricity. Imagination brings a building into being, an imagination that operates for each person involved in this work, from inception to final touch of paint.

We use our imagination so often and so naturally, that we tend to lose sight of the magic of what we are doing. Furthermore, it is difficult to describe the connection between work and imagination in a way that is not circular, because whatever we decide constitutes our work is itself the product of our imagination. Every day, each one of us creatively perceives the possibilities in the moment, and, for some of us, those imaginings are wonderfully open. Others of us are more limited in our imagination, confining our mental pictures to a close approximation of what we experienced yesterday. But in both cases, we are creating a new world in our imagination. We are, whether we know it or not, picturing the birth of a new and different world, and then acting to make that picture a reality.

Thus, we can see why our imagination is so important to soul work. If we want to engage the world out of the depths of our core values and identity, it we must first *imagine* out of those same depths.

This means that our first action as we set about bringing our souls to work must be to ask, "Are we imagining rightly? Do we have an accurate vision of what we could do? Do we have a clear perspective on where our work can take us?" As we become right in our imagination, our work will automatically start to adjust and begin to meet our souls.

Intentions

As we all know, however, imagination is not enough to get anything done; we all imagine many things, but only engage in a few. I may imagine the great novel I want to write, but until I take the step of *intending* to write that novel, it will never be. I may imagine ways of making the world a better place, but until I *intend* to carry out those plans, the world will not change (at least not as a result of my imagining). Intention is the "will" that leads to action; of all these things that *could* be, this is what I *will* do!

The thing about our intentions is that they are never entirely clear or pure. Much has been written and said about how our intentions flow out of the more "primitive" aspects of our existence. From the Buddha to Sigmund Freud, we find out that what we *intend* generally reflects something deep inside us. This means, for example, that if we imagine a variety of ways to improve the world, those which we actually move into the realm of intention will likely be the ones that also carry something else, and often that something else is a deep and powerful self-interest. Our intentions carry our deepest fears, our anxieties, our most profound hopes, and our core convictions about what *must* be. So we must monitor our intentions, seeking to understand what they will bring to life, and cautioning ourselves that our intentions never reflect *only* the purest and best part of ourselves.

Our intentions must also find a harmony with the environment within which we work. As a hairstylist, I may want to produce good-looking-customers, but I also have an idea in my own mind of what a good looking customer looks like, an idea which may not be shared by my customer. As the customer service revolution has tried to point out, a good intention, at least in part, is one which the *customer* perceives as good, and that is not always the same as what I, the worker, intend. To make matters more complex, few of us work solely on the basis of our own intentions. Those of us who work for other people are particularly dependent upon the intentions of others. And they in turn are dependent upon other people's intentions. The web of intentions stretches out in long and confusing strands. So now our intentions are becoming complex entities, a composition of our desires and our environment.

However, we need not follow this confusing web to the point of certainty. For one thing, we cannot. There is never certainty when it comes to human intentions. The most important thing is to make a serious effort to *attend* to our own intentions. We can attend, and insist that, as far as possible, the intention behind our work is the creation of a better world. We can look at ourselves in the mirror and be clear that, through our work, we want to see the world become a cleaner, healthier place, where good relationships flourish and where people are able to grow in their capacities.

The key point is to question our intentions in the first place. If all we are after is money or an easy time, we will know it. And if we are trying to build a better world through what we do, we will know that too. We will never know with absolute certainty, which means that we can never stop asking the question, but we can know with enough clarity that we can either continue what we are doing, or know that our intentions need to change.

The other aspect of intentions is planning. Good intentions are mapped and organized to accomplish goals. We need to be clear about *what* we intend to do, as well as *when* and *how* we intend to do it, in order to accomplish soul work. Without a plan, our good intentions get squandered in frustrated aimlessness. It is not that we do not know what we want to accomplish, but that we do not know what route to take. Planning, of course, can be a form of work all its own. Planning is a major supervisory task. Yet it is also something each of us needs to do. We *all* need to have a plan, even if our only goal is to be a nicer person.

Our intentions must also find a harmony with the environment within which we work.

Skill

A skill is something we use to make our intentions a reality. Without skills, intentions remain just that – good intentions. We use skills to turn the resources we work with into products. We may have the highly sophisticated skills of a software engineer, or the simple skills of a parking lot attendant.

Skills are something we possess to either a greater or lesser degree. I once had the opportunity to work with a group of highly skilled individuals on a very complex project, which had to be completed within a very short time frame. It was a wonderful experience. We did good work, and we got it done with tremendous satisfaction along the way. I have also worked with task groups who were not adequately skilled. We still managed to get the work done, but it was not as pleasurable, nor was the outcome as good. It was not bad work, but it was a long way from what a better trained group could have accomplished. Good work requires good skills.

This brings us to *mastery*. It used to be that workers were divided into three categories: apprentices, journeymen, and masters. The apprentice was a person who was actively learning a trade. The journeyman was one who had gained enough skill that they could work on their own. The master, however, not only understood the traditional ways of working and could execute them with ease, but could even produce entirely new ways of working. The master was the one who was sought for teaching or whenever something new was encountered. Masters were those for whom the skills had become a full extension of their being. In our world we have generally forgotten this concept. We see a world in flux and change, so we do not want to settle into anything fully. Likewise, if we are to access the full potential of our work, sometimes we must be prepared to pursue mastery. In the next chapter we will explore fully the impact of this possibility.

It may be worth adding that good tools go hand in hand with good skills. Without tools, skills cannot be used. With *good* tools, good skills become excellence applied. The better the tools, the better the work.

Effort

No work takes place without effort. It takes energy, drive, and commitment to do soul work. Those who do not bring these things will fall short, produce sub-standard or less-than-excellent products. Soul work requires that we reach into ourselves and put our very essence into our tasks. Generally, this means approaching our work with enthusiasm, looking for every opportunity to achieve or improve upon our best.

In every case, effort takes something from us. While soul work puts energy into the universe, it also takes energy out of us. Ideally, our efforts will trigger a substantial change in the energy flow of those around us, through our work outcomes. If this trigger effect does not happen, if we feel as if we are pushing against a weight that won't budge, then we may need to re-examine our work.

And yet, we also often encounter a threshold effect: a little bit of effort does not succeed (or feel very good), but more effort does. I am not suggesting that we wear or burn ourselves out, but I do know that the best work almost always happens only after sustained effort; it happens after we have begun to feel "stretched." It can be as simple as the glow that comes from sustained physical exertion, or as complex as the release that comes from working many hours at a complex problem.

Even so, work always requires rest. We need a "Sabbath," a point where we say, "We must rest from our labors" – even though those labors may be very good. Failure to rest, no matter how good and exciting our work, is a dangerous act.

Ideally, our efforts will trigger a substantial change in the energy flow of those around us, through our work outcomes.

In the best situations, the effort we apply resonates deep inside ourselves, with a harmonic effect that allows our effort to *sing*. We know we have found our soul work when, as we begin to struggle to get things done, part of us says back to us "For this we were made!" Obviously, this does not mean, that soul work is easy, only that there is a powerful "rightness" to it that is revealed as we do it.

Resources

Resources are the things we convert, under the direction of intentions, through the application of skills and effort, into the products of our work. The hairstylist's resources are the customer's hair, the dyes, shampoos, electricity, and water he uses. The urban planner's resources are the focus groups, the engineering studies, the demographic projections, and the council meetings. Each converts their resources into products. No matter what sort of work we do, there are resources – inputs – which we convert into outputs of products and services.

The quality of resources available to us can vary greatly. The best work requires good resources. Sometimes this quality can be difficult to ascertain, because it is only through the work itself that we come to know the quality of our resources. But we do learn, and then are able to find better resources.

When it comes to resources, there exists a special category of work and workers – those who make "more" out of "less." This is especially worth recognizing in a world of dwindling resources, where resources need to be shared more equitably. Making more out of less means there is more to go around. It usually also leads to fewer negative by-products, such as waste or pollution.

Process

A process is the directed and organized flow of all of the above, and while it may not look like a thing in itself, there is something very special happening here. Processes occur in and over time, and time itself is the marker of a journey. It is in the process of work that we journey from this world into the future.

Journeys, of course, can happen many ways. No matter how well-prepared we are, we may find that our journey, once begun, brings the completely unexpected. Or it may unfold exactly as we have projected. But in any journey things are set in motion and so we always face a pregnant future: one our work will birth.

There are also, of course, better and worse ways of journeying. Our processes can be more or less than adequate for the work we are trying to accomplish. Our goal is to use the best processes we can, to most smoothly, efficiently, cooperatively, and effectively bring our products into existence.

Products

Products are the most complex part of the work model. They are complex not only because they reflect the intentions, skill, effort, and resources that went into them, a complex enough equation to begin with, but because once they have been produced they take on a life of their own. Once a product becomes available, it can be used by others to do things that may not reflect the goodness that went into its production. Or it can be used to do things much better than any use the worker could have imagined. The pickup truck used to transport food to famine stricken areas is doing a good work and fulfilling a goodness of which its assemblers may have had no conception. The razor sharp cooking knife used to threaten a co-worker is a danger and not the excellent tool its manufacturer intended. This complexity cannot be managed. A product, once it is produced, moves outside our control. We cannot know if our products will be used well or poorly, within the range intended, or in some other unimagined way.

When bad uses of our product take place, we must ask ourselves, "Could we have produced this product in such a way that this bad use was impossible, or less likely?"

However, even though we cannot know with certainty how our products will be used, our responsibility does not end once the product is completed. When bad uses of our product take place, we must ask ourselves, "Could we have produced this product in such a way that this bad use was impossible, or less likely?" This question must be directed at each step of the way: Could we have imagined better? Could we have intended better? Could we have been more skillful? Could we have applied more effort? Could we have used better resources, or used our existing resources better? Ideally, a bad use of our product becomes the opportunity to improve our product. Bad uses can be a critical spur to "better" work. Similarly, keep looking for new and positive uses; they speak of new opportunities and potentials. Perhaps with only small changes, we could make those unexpected good uses better, or come up with entirely new products or services that make the world a better place.

We also need to take into account the decay process as the product or service reaches the end of its life. An excellent haircut is one that continues to stay neat even as the hair becomes longer and shaggier. A PCB-filled electrical transformer reveals its nature as a bad work only when it reaches the end of its life and becomes a health hazard. How a product leaves the cycle of existence tells us as much about the work that led to it as anything else about it. A city plan that continues to enlighten and promote a healthy vision of the city, even as its projections become out of date, is an excellent one and demonstrates the full goodness of the work that went into it.

Classic products are those we look back upon as milestones, special markers of the excellence of our work.

Ideally, good products become "classic" products. Classic products are those we look back upon as milestones, special markers of the excellence of our work. These become both points of tremendous satisfaction (especially when others recognize the value of that special product) and the standards of excellence for our work and the future work of others. Classics are not just better; they stand for the *best* that could be done and point the way for other *excellent* products.

By-products

By-products are the inherent, positive or negative secondary outcomes produced through our work. A paycheck is a *positive* by-product, which most of us receive due to our work. Other positive by-products include the satisfaction and esteem our work may generate. At the same time, our work always produces *negative* by-products. This is one of the fundamental laws of the universe. Waste, for example, is a negative by-product of all work. Observing these by-products and evaluating them in relation to our products is something that must take place at all times.

Unintended Consequences

An elderly acquaintance of mine, a retired executive of a major corporation, talks regularly about the Law of Unintended Consequences. After many years of work, he concluded that no matter what else happens, there will always be unexpected side effects. Sometimes these fall into the "I *should* have known" category. And sometimes they fall into the "I *wish* I had known" category. But most often, they fall into the "How on Earth did that happen!?" category. No matter how carefully we plan or work things through beforehand, we should always expect unexpected consequences. Things happen.

A CEO once told me about a personality dispute among his board of directors that kept him from being able to focus on the long-term good of the company. He also told me about how he had straightened out the relationships, enabling him to get on with his job more effectively. He subsequently left the organization and I came in to do some work for them (based on his recommendation). What surprised me, given my past conversations with him, was that things were far from the happy state he recounted. Even more, I saw that there were serious problems at the upper levels of the organization. Though it was not my responsibility, my position gave me access to information on the board of directors. I saw that while it was indeed true that the old pattern of hostility was no longer present, in solving the problem, the former CEO had inadvertently changed the dynamics of the board, such that they began to interfere in the life of the organization and made the life of subsequent senior management hellish. The unintended consequences of the "solution" created brand new and much more serious problems.

Unintended consequences come from two sources. The first is ignorance. Often, we could have projected the consequences if we had been more experienced, better informed, better trained, or more alert. Not surprisingly, these consequences also reflect our unexamined intentions, those deep parts of us that hide within our motivations and only emerge after the fact. If we had known ourselves better, we would have seen what was going to happen. This problem diminishes with time, as we come to know better through experience.

The second source of unintended consequences is something called "sensitive dependence upon initial conditions," or more simply "chaos." The world is not stable. Everything is connected to everything else, in ways far beyond our ability to perceive, let alone control. So when we undertake any action it always acts as a trigger to other things – unexpected things, unanticipated things. These unintended consequences are the natural consequence of our complex interconnections as people, organizations, ecologies, and structures.

After years of observing and consulting for organizations, I am convinced that the law of unintended consequences does not treat all outcomes equally.

The law of unintended consequences means that, as we work, we must always pay close attention to what is happening "behind our shoulders," so to speak. We need to scan the environment diligently, looking for those places where our work is creating major change in unexpected places. As we work, we need to be prepared to stop or change direction, as unintended consequences roll out around us.

Buried inside the law of unintended consequences is something else, something that speaks to me of hope in the very structure of the universe. After years of observing and consulting for organizations, I am convinced that the law of unintended consequences does not treat all outcomes equally. *Negative* unintended consequences are less common than *positive* unintended consequences. Further, positive unintended consequences seem more likely to occur when those involved are *positive* in their outlook themselves. Time and again (but not always) I see negative unintended consequences grind to a halt before long. Time and again (but not always) I see positive unintended consequences continue to radiate out in ways that trigger more positive consequences. This happens around *positively* oriented people, because they inherently trigger better things in minute ways all the time, creating a kind of field of positive opportunity.

I have seen it so often that I am convinced it is a natural law of the universe itself: good stuff (usually) grows; bad stuff (usually) dies.

Learning

One of the most important outcomes of all work is learning. We, and the work systems of which we are a part, gain knowledge and experience through every act of work we undertake. We become able to see more clearly, project more effectively, work more skillfully, based on our past doings. This feedback effect means that, as things move along, we typically get better at what we do. Sometimes this is the most important product of our work, as, for example, when we learn that we have natural abilities in a certain field and can thus focus more of ourselves within it. This kind of learning doesn't just happen at the individual level, it also happens at the organizational level, and within society as a whole.

Opportunity

I have left for last what I have come to think is the most important aspect of work: the field of opportunity within which it takes place. Intentions take us to a critical point, but if we are to engage in our work we must have a "field of opportunity" within which to ply our skills, where the resources are available, and where processes can take place. In many respects, this field of opportunity is what leads to work, sustains our work, and even redeems our work if it goes wrong. If we lose our field of opportunity, we cease to be able to work. If we find new opportunity, we can do new work. Depending on the opportunity, our work will take one form and not another.

By field of opportunity, I mean the web of connections that make work possible. None of us engages in work by ourselves. Our portion fits into the work of many others, and into their expectations, possibilities, desires, and outcomes. While our imagination and intentions are our own, we learn skills through training and work, both of which depend on others.

What we seek to do must be in harmony with the imagination, intentions, and resources of those who make the opportunity possible.

The resources we use are often the product of other people's work, something other people have made available to us. And finally, the processes we use require a context that permits them to be sustained. If our work causes a change in the environment that then eliminates the opportunity, we will be forced to cease our work. Consider, for example, a youngster making mud pies who is abruptly interrupted by a horrified parent. The field of opportunity for that child is eliminated simply because the child undertook the work in front of his or her parent.

This means that a positive resonance must exist between us and the field of opportunity that surrounds us, as a prerequisite of soul work. What we seek to do must be in harmony with the imagination, intentions, and resources of those who make the opportunity possible; if it is not, we will not be given the opportunity, or we will find that the opportunity is diminished or eliminated. On the other hand, if what we seek to do *is* in harmony with the field of opportunity, then it will become more fully available to us.

There are two other aspects to this harmony that have a bearing on soul-based work. First, we should recognize that we may experience harmony at some levels, and not at others; in some parts of our existence, and not in others. Even though we may resonate with certain aspects of an opportunity, there may be other pieces necessary to the opportunity with which we do *not* resonate.

An example: A friend was recently talking to a potential employer about a job. Her skills, experience, and commitments exactly matched what the employer was looking for – something they both recognized as they talked with each other. The needs of each fit at every level they could discover, a resonance that excited both of them. Then my friend started to think about some of the commitments in her private life and she realized that if she took this job, aspects of her private life could become deeply embarrassing to her future employer. When she discussed this with the employer, they assured her that this would not be the case. Still, as she thought about it, she realized she would end up in a position of divided loyalties. While she supported this organization wholeheartedly, she knew her other commitments could potentially cause trouble, which would mean she would always have this worry hanging over her work. She decided to end the discussions. For her, the potential dissonance at one level overwhelmed the resonance at other levels.

Every field of opportunity has a built-in directional flow, which, once we accept or engage with the opportunity, will begin to shape us.

The second aspect we need to attend to is one my friend successfully avoided: that is, the temptation to settle for only *partial* resonance, and to close our eyes to where the opportunity may be leading us. Every field of opportunity has a built-in directional flow, which, once we accept or engage with the opportunity, will begin to shape us. It is like a fast moving current in a stream. The water may look inviting on a hot day, but once we step into it, the current will push us downstream.

An opportunity can mean so much to us, especially when it tugs at many parts of our being. But it can also lead us down paths we should not travel, paths that lead us away from the things that are most important to us. What would have happened to my friend had she taken the job? Would she have ended up backing away from her other commitments, in order to keep her employer happy? Or would she have started covering things up? Or perhaps started deceiving herself? All of these are possible, and all of them would have had a negative impact on her.

The power of a field of opportunity is so great we may not even sense what is happening and may be taken away by it and transformed into very different people. If it is a positive field, one we have explored and in which we have found great resonance at many levels, then we will become better people. If it is not resonant with us, is not headed in a direction we should travel, then sooner or later we will find ourselves facing difficult decisions about who we are and what we are doing with our lives.

Putting all these things together, from imagination to unintended consequences, and placing them within a field of opportunity, we can see just how complicated work actually is. And yet we work every day, involved, enmeshed, and engaged in the creation of a new universe; transforming today into tomorrow; reaching with our souls to birth the future. No matter how complicated the reality, this is what we do. And when we understand that, then we can do better – and we can always do better. Even more importantly, we can *be* better. Knowing what we are doing, we can become better people.

Room for Improvement

If we look at each of these pieces, we can see that, usually, there will be room for improvement. Certainly, many of us return from our work deeply satisfied with what we are producing and who we are becoming. But many others of us come away from our work dissatisfied with both. We know that our work reflects less than our best and that what we produce through our work should be better than it is. Our task, on our soul's journey, is to achieve, to the greatest extent possible, the former.

Defining our work in this way puts a tremendous responsibility on our shoulders. Whether soul work happens in the world is in large measure up to us. While we may sometimes feel constrained by our world, we are not held captive by it. Ideally, as we examine each of the parts of our work, we will find that we are proud of the work we are doing. I suspect, however, that most of us find that as we struggle to do good work, there will always be things we can improve. We can allow ourselves more "free" space and time to imagine creatively. We can be clearer about our intentions. We can develop our skills. We can apply more consistent effort. We can select better resources. We can refine the product, or change some of the by-products. There is almost always something we can do better. This, too, is part of soul work and we can take pride in our drive to improve.

Putting all these things together, from imagination to unintended consequences, and placing them within a field of opportunity, we can see just how complicated work actually is.

As great as this responsibility is, it should not feel like a burden. Rare is the person who wakes up to what they are doing and mourns. Most of us want to improve, are always seeking to improve, and will improve. Furthermore, my experience suggests that most people naturally begin to change in small increments, not all at once.

In addition, once we focus on improvement in even the smallest of things, we find that those around us start to change. When one person starts to do better, everyone else finds it easier to do better too, and things begin to spiral out in a cycle of goodness. Good work leads to better work and better work leads to the best work – our soul work. Most of us *want* to find and do our soul work, and when faced with someone who has directly taken on that challenge, we find it easier to embrace the challenge ourselves.

Of course, there are always a few who will see our attempt to do our soul work as a criticism or a violation, and who will attempt to make things worse. Many a young worker, full of zeal, has faced the displeasure of older workers used to other ways, or a less productive pace. Regardless, those who are intent on doing their soul work focus on *remaining* soul workers, taking whatever comes their way as a resource in their struggle to make themselves better. By doing so, they help others move further along a path that leads to their own soul work. Often, too, the opposition we face is far shallower than it feels, though not always – trying to do your soul work can get you fired. The way of the soul is, ultimately, the way of all people. It is just that, sometimes, the old ways are hard to outgrow.

Soul work is the end *and the* means. *It is both the* goal *toward which we strive and the* method *by which we achieve it.*

In all of this, I have been trying to show that soul work is the *end* and the *means*. It is both the *goal* toward which we strive and the *method* by which we achieve it. We all want to find the point where we can say with satisfaction, "Well done." But even to strive to find that continually shifting point is to do soul work. Every step, every effort, puts in front of us and others a new target, a new hope, a new possibility. Every step, every effort, is part of the journey of our soul.

However, not all souls take the same path. There are at least two different ways in which souls journey. It is to these two paths, and their implications for our work, that we turn next.

4

Working Souls
The Experience of Work

There exist, in my experience, two basic arcs to the soul and subsequently two basic ways we do our work. These two arcs are the way of the *master* and the way of the *savior*. The way of the master is the way of the one who seeks to understand and move within the flow of existence. The way of the savior is the way of the one who seeks to understand and decisively *alter* the flow of existence.

Consider two friends of mine, one the minister of a local church and the other a wealthy entrepreneur. The minister has been at his church for about 15 years, a very long time when you consider that most of the other churches in the area have had two or three ministers during the same period. He has also become a highly respected person in the church nationally and internationally. On the other hand, the entrepreneur is busy raking in (and losing) millions of dollars,

The way of the master is the way of the one who seeks to understand and move within the flow of existence. The way of the savior is the way of the one who seeks to understand and decisively alter the flow of existence.

leaping rapidly from opportunity to opportunity, exploiting each one to its fullest before moving on.

The minister is a *master*. He does little, says little, and listens much. When he does do something, he does it tentatively, carefully, and cautiously. At one time, I found him very frustrating to work with; from my perspective, it seemed as though nothing much happened. Except that one does not gain his kind of reputation, or survive the kind of crises he had faced, unless there is something very powerful going on.

Over the years, I have come to understand a little of how he works. The secret to his approach, I believe, is that he stands within the energies of the people systems that are his life, and maneuvers himself in tiny ways, such that the forces of the systems shift around him. And good things happen – but slowly, unfolding like a flower, one petal at a time.

The entrepreneur, on the other hand, is a *savior*. She has a roving eye for opportunities. When she sees something she believes is worth working at, she moves decisively and strongly, applying her full attention and resources, concerned only with what it takes to succeed.

My description of these two people is almost a caricature, but, in truth, they are each spiritually committed, hard working, and doing their best to do make the world a better place. (And of the two, I think the minister is the better business person.) They illustrate two very different ways of acting powerfully in our world, ways I have come to see as distinct and often misunderstood. Yet they appeal to each of us in different measure, and each of us will seek to emulate them more strongly in one way than another. We need to understand the "why" of each of these folk, in order to understand our own soul work, and how it will become *ours* and no one else's.

Masters

We are surrounded by forces that shape our existence. They were here before we came along and they will be here long after we are gone. Some of these forces come from the economic and social structures in which we live. Some of them ebb and flow with life itself. And some of them swirl just out of sight in the fundamental nature of existence itself. These forces are always moving, and the patterns of their movement can be discerned by the more sensitive among us. For the rest of us, they just *are* – sometimes confusing, sometimes clear, but always carrying us along.

The future we create will not break the flow, but will work with the energies of the flow to enhance and improve what is always fundamentally there.

For some of us, our work will call us to attend closely to these forces. We will develop listening ears, open hearts, and gentle fingertips, as we work to move with these forces in order to accomplish that which we see needs doing. The future we create will not break the flow, but will work with the energies of the flow to enhance and improve what is always fundamentally there. And, as we immerse ourselves within these forces, we will find ourselves being transformed. We will move from gawky apprentice, to skilled crafter, to powerful master. My minister friend, from many years of experience, knows how to bend and manipulate symbols so that the natural energies in people and organizations find constructive places to engage each other and the world. He is indeed a master.

But the way of the master is not a way of life that attracts us all. In times of crisis or substantial change, there seems to be little value in the master's bending and flexing before the currents. During such times, the actions of the master can seem like muddling and stumbling, rather than the decisive action the events appear to call for. My friend the minister has been accused of hypocrisy and worse, for his flexible approach to things. Typically, these accusations come from folk who prefer the other basic arc.

Saviors

Saviors are also sensitive, in their own way, to the forces around us, but they have a very different pattern of existence in mind. They notice how forces come together to mark specific, real and potential transitions, and how new possibilities can be created, if the forces are shifted. They see not just a world of flow, but a world where specific and accurately focused actions, taking the right form in the right place at the right time, can completely change the world. They realize that it is possible – if you know how to act correctly, and do so – to alter the patterns of force or energy permanently, and in the interests of one or more parties active in the flow.

We seek out those places where we can change the structure of our existence, through our innovations and personal contributions.

This is a path to which others of us, such as my entrepreneur friend, are called. We seek out those places where we can change the structure of our existence, through our innovations and personal contributions. We feel best when we bring our creative energies and skill to bear on a fulcrum in the forces that shape the world around us. Once we find that point, we focus everything we have on it, exert every effort, with the goal of ensuring that our work will take us through that transition.

For those of us who take this route, it is not to be a slow progression from apprentice to master, through immersion in our work. The point, for us, is to make a decisive change, at a specific point, using the resources at our disposal at that time. We "fish the world" trying to maximize the full range of learning in each situation, so that when we see the point of change, we are able to act effectively. Usually we gravitate toward work where these types of shifts happen most easily, or to places where there are others like us, who will appreciate our "revolutionary" commitment and approach to work.

Decision Making

Given the above, we have some choices to face and decisions to make. Each of us has a natural affinity for one of these two ways of working. We will tend to choose the either the path of the master or the path of the savior. We will make this choice based on who we are, what we have experienced in life, and what we believe most deeply about ourselves. And while we may (at our best) admire the "other" way of *being* in work, deep inside ourselves we will *know* that one way is truer than the other, *for us*. That is *our* way of being in our work.

Of course, this means that no matter which choice we make, we will find at times that our work calls for the other approach and that we are out of sorts, so to speak. Masters become lost in times of revolutionary change and must uncharacteristically make strong transformations. Saviors become lost in times of slow change, where careful attention to the natural flow is the required way and therefore must uncharacteristically cease their movement. And always, some of us are more flexible than others.

North America has favored the savior mode of being for most of its history. In part, this has been due to the Puritan/Protestant ethic that underlies mainstream North American culture. And, in part, it has been due to the incredible growth and wealth of opportunity within North America. That wealth has also made it easy to overlook the mistakes made by this mode.

Currently, however, we are becoming aware that the ecological well-being of our world requires a more sensitive approach, one that works within the framework of the existing natural forces. A larger and more complex culture made up of many peoples also requires that we increase our sensitivity to each other and to the patterns of our collective existence. And, finally, we are becoming aware that the mistakes made by those in the savior mode can inadvertently push us "over the edge," through economically, politically, or environmentally destructive behavior.

On the other hand, this does not mean that we must, or are able to, become a culture of masters. Both masters and saviors bring powerful and useful perspectives. We must simply live, sometimes uncomfortably, in the tension between these two. And we must, therefore, more carefully attend to the forces in the midst of existence. We must remain fast on our feet and ready to innovate. Given the tremendous complexity of contemporary existence and in many cases the difficulty of accurately assessing what type of work our situation calls for, we must sometimes agree to disagree with each other over when each mode is called for, and how it is called for, and to what degree. But I hope that we can at least come to admire the successes each approach brings.

We live in a world where both arcs exist powerfully. Genuine masters always believe, deep inside themselves, that releasing ego identity and immersing the self in the well-being of the whole will gently shift existence itself towards the necessary good. And that is exactly what happens. At the same time, genuine saviors always believe, deep inside themselves, that maximizing ego identity and using all of it to transform the world for the well-being of the whole will radically shift existence towards the necessary good. And that, too, is exactly what happens. Each of us must choose the arc we will call our own, and, once chosen, that arc will structure our path in ways that cannot be altered.

Arcs within Frameworks

Having made that fundamental choice, or more likely, having found that choice already made deep inside us, we still face many other decisions. Regardless of our arc, we must make our way through the myriad aspects of work itself, seeking within our arc to ensure that our daily work takes us appropriately to our soul work. From imagination through final consequences, our work forces us to make decisions that will emerge from and reflect our arc. It is in the totality of our engagement with existence, through the results of many decisions in the midst of our specific field of opportunity, that we come to know our own soul work.

My conviction rests on the assumption that soul work doesn't get done by happenstance. We need to be able to sense or see, as we engage in action, how our behavior will lead to a better world, or how our behavior may lead to something less desirable. Regardless of our arc, some actions simply *are* better than others; some actions will shift us more effectively into the egoless-ness that will lead to good, and some actions will allow us to more effectively apply our skills and resources to creating decisive change. Which are those actions? And how do we know when we are following the best course for our arc?

Regardless of how difficult our work situation is, how oppressive the conditions or management, our soul's arc can direct and help us to a better future.

There are a number of points to take into consideration as we try to answer these questions. First, we must note that our journey never follows a straight line. We must accept that there will be divergences, "learning experiences," and trade-offs along the way. Life is complex and, as we make our way, we will find ourselves being forced to adjust our course to the circumstances. Therefore, we will need to have both a long- and a short-term vision for our actions. And we will need to have alternative strategies to assist us when things go wrong.

In this context, it may be important to stress that *everyone* is capable of finding soul work. Regardless of how difficult our work situation is, how oppressive the conditions or management, our soul's arc can direct and help us to a better future. It can be something as small as being polite to others and helping each other to see the humanity we share. Even if all we do is tighten bolts on an assembly line, we are doing right work if our goal is to produce a more reliable and trustworthy product, and to build healthy relationships with our peers and supervisors. Even in that restricted environment, we will find the power of mastery, or the opportunity for radical change. There is no place where soul work cannot happen as we each make use of the opportunities and options we have to move toward the best in our situation.

Paradoxically, many of us face the opposite difficulty. In our culture of wealth and possibility, many of us face not a limited range of possibilities, but an overabundance of possibilities. The challenge for many of us – and it's a tough one – is not choosing between good and evil, or detecting the forces of harmony in the midst of discord, but determining the "better" from the many "goods." We can easily find ourselves throwing up our hands in confusion and dismay as we try to choose the "best" work.

There are indicators that help us to know whether our path is correct. These indicators are labor *and* toil. *Both of these indicators are our emotional and psychological response to our experience of our work.*

Time plays a role here as well. We are caught within time, struggling with our past and our sense of the future; or, to put it more clearly, what has happened to us in the past will have a very large influence on how we see the future. This creates a basic flaw in our perspective (no matter what our arc) that is difficult to ameliorate. If the future can be radically different from the past (as it can be) then we are at a certain level always unprepared for it.

To make our way easier, then, we must find an internal "compass." We must find those indicators that tell us where we are going, and whether in the moment, we are in the right place. I believe there are indicators that help us to know whether our path is correct. These indicators are *labor* and *toil*. Both of these indicators are our emotional and psychological response to our experience of our work.

Each of us experiences work differently based on our abilities, personality, experience, needs, state of development, goals, and soul arc. Work that I find immensely satisfying, my "soul work," may be work that drives you to frustration, and the reverse may also be true. We are each different and experience work differently. And yet, within that diversity of experience, lie two core experiences. Specifically, most of us experience work as either *labor* or *toil*. If we understand them, these two experiences can help us know whether our work is right for us.

Labor

Sometimes, we experience work as labor. And labor is something positive. Think of how we use the term in speech. We often speak of a "labor of love." We also refer to a woman's effort in childbirth as labor. This latter example illustrates especially well the unique character of labor.

Creativity, relational sensitivity, and insight are important parts of many jobs and these things emerge from who we are and what we believe about the world.

Labor refers to the effort we expend and the opportunity we have to express ourselves and our convictions through our work. It is the part of work that is shaped by, and in some measure reflects, our identity. Each of us, no matter how routine or standardized our work, leaves a mark, a trace of our passing on our work. Labor is also our experience of living through our work. When we labor, we find ourselves giving life to something important to us. When we end our labor it is with satisfaction.

This is most obvious for those who work in jobs where the human component is central. Creativity, relational sensitivity, and insight are important parts of many jobs and these things emerge from who we are and what we believe about the world. The doctor's "bedside manner" is a key part of how she heals. The sales person puts himself into the relationship with the customer. The work of the artist or architect, strategic planner or writer, all show the signs of their creator's vision, personality, beliefs, and energy. Those with the opportunity to do these kinds of work sometimes find in their labor something almost transcendent, an experience of creator and cosmos moving into harmony.

But labor is also present in more technical jobs. The mechanic demonstrates a way of working with parts or the house painter uses a quality of paint and craftsmanship that reflect his understanding of quality. I once had a mechanic who was someone special. He exuded a love of motors and a concern for cars as he worked. I knew that, when he was done, my car had been worked on not only by someone with technical ability, but by someone with a deep commitment to the well-being of my car. I remember that he once dragged me from one car to the next in the shop, showing me the various components, explaining the costs of various parts, and how he worked to ensure that the cars worked well at the lowest cost to their owners. Competent car repair I can get at many garages, but this level of commitment is something for which I would willingly pay extra. His work was genuine labor.

If I know that a little extra care in my work can be an expression of my belief in caring for the world, I will feel better about my work and, in many cases, others will feel better about me, too.

Even in rote manufacturing, labor is involved. In simple assembly-line, nuts-and-bolts work, there is labor. An angry person will cross thread more, have a generally lower level of productivity, and be harder to work with than will someone who puts their will and happiness into the job. We always have the opportunity to express a little of who we are and what we believe in our work.

Knowing that we labor can be liberating. Once we know that we always have an impact through the effort we put in, we can strive to maximize that impact. When I know that my smile changes the situation, I can improve my work by smiling more frequently. If I know that a little extra care in my work can be an expression of my belief in caring for the world, I will feel better about my work and, in many cases, others will feel better about me, too. When we are able release our inner beings into the labor of our work, we have the potential to become one with our work.

While the examples above seem to privilege the path of the *master*, the experience of labor is just as much a possibility for those who follow the path of the savior. Watching carefully for the most effective points of intervention can be done in many ways, and when our daily work is done with grace, clarity, and wholeness of being, new doors will open and new transformations will become possible. It is not a matter of only waiting for the right moment; it is also a matter of striving at all times to confront the forces of existence with commitment, and to prepare the conditions for positive transformation. If we do this, we will find that at even those points where total transformation is necessary, we will act with greater peace, wholeness, and clarity.

I believe that the possibility of labor is an expression of the presence of love in the universe. It means that no matter where we are, no matter what our circumstances, we can make a genuine impact for the better. Through our labor, we give birth to a profoundly better world, and we, in turn, are humanized and enabled to grow.

Toil

There is another side to the experience of work. Regardless of who we are, how sainted we might be, or what we do, part of our work hurts us. That destruction may be done to ourselves – physically, mentally, or spiritually – or to those around us, or to the planet itself. There is a part of what we do that makes us and the world worse. This is the tragedy of work. This is toil.

We all experience part of our work as a "grind," as difficult, as a struggle, or as something hurtful. It can be something as little as having to show up for work on a regular basis; for some of us, routine is very hard to take. For others, it may be that their workplace is an abusive, soul destroying combination of anger, poor working conditions, waste, and danger.

One of the terrible ironies for those in the helping professions, particularly for therapists, is that they must sometimes assist in destruction in order to build. To help a person with a damaged inner being to recover, they must sometimes walk alongside as their client destroys relationships, hurts those close to them, and suffers great agonies. A journey of healing can leave great damage in its wake, a damage which the therapist feels and sometimes finds personally destructive.

The negative consequences of toil can be extreme. Some bosses work their staff to destruction, bullying and preying on psychological weakness until their employees are ready to break. Some jobs simply demand so much of people that they are unable to contribute to their families, friends, or communities. Some jobs prey on customers, exploiting their weaknesses for money. Some jobs leave immense ecological destruction in their wake. The toil here infects whole communities.

Sometimes the toil is due to who we are in our work. While I was a graduate student, I spent four years working part-time as a clerk in a library. The job paid well and gave me time to work on my thesis and attend classes. It was an excellent situation for any student. But it also ground me down. There was no activity that was not written down in the operations manual or scheduled down to the minute. The routine was immense and stultifying. I experienced the lack of opportunity to contribute or change things as a prison. After four years, the stress was almost intolerable and I suffered some obvious side effects. But my personality was the major factor here, not something inherent in the job. I worked in a department of four and at least two of the other three staff enjoyed their work immensely. These two showed an enthusiasm for the routine that amazed me. They obviously enjoyed what they did and where they did it. Clearly, what made that job toil for me was a combination of my personality, my expectations, and my place in the world. I am an imaginative, creative person. I love change. I treasure the opportunity to contribute new ideas and methods. Closely managed, routine work is something I will always experience as toil.

In contrast, I have noticed that the working conditions under which I thrive – high stress, deadline ridden, development filled, and cutting edge – are conditions that many people find very difficult. What sends me humming to sleep is enough to drive some up the walls. They experience as toil something I would not trade for anything.

This can be taken as an excuse for wishing we were other than we are, for trying to match our personalities to our work. But I believe it is easier and better to change the type of work we do so that it matches the type of people we are. Our work should not leave us angry at the end of each day. It should not bring us down. It should not be overwhelming emotional toil. Our work should not destroy us.

> *Our work should not leave us angry at the end of each day. It should not bring us down. It should not be overwhelming emotional toil. Our work should not destroy us.*

Even so, the best work will have some element of toil, just as the worst work has some element of labor. Soul work usually has less toil than labor. But both labor and toil are present in differing degrees, degrees known only to each of us. They are the *experience* of work.

Vocation

One final way of thinking about work which we need to examine before we can go on is that of vocation. For centuries, people have had "vocations," work they experienced as a *calling* and that was understood to be a lifelong commitment. Today we live in a world where the idea of *belonging to your work* seems ridiculous. At the same time, very little is permanent, and very few types of work will last as long as we will. It seems that the concept of vocation is obsolete.

Yet we cannot put the concept aside. Every so often I find, even in our chaotic world, people who have found their vocation, their sacred calling. Generally, these are folk who are so immersed in their work that they cannot imagine doing anything else. I know a few teachers like that. I suspect my mechanic, mentioned above, is another such person. I see in these folk a kind of serenity, a being at peace.

I know other people who strive to find their vocation. They search for the work of their hearts, the place where they can apply their energy with the knowledge that of the many possibilities in the universe, this is the one *to which they belong*. Some find it. But others do not. I do not think that this failure is necessarily their own; it is often due to the nature of life itself. Life is an inherently and continuously shifting collection of experiences and opportunities, a web of unceasing possibility, where we move along lines partly of our own volition, and partly at the hands of those around us (our personal field of opportunity). The conditions may never arise where we find the exact place we belong. Therefore, to live well and effectively in the midst of life, we need to be able to maintain balance, seeing both the good possibilities and the bad possibilities around us in the moment itself. As long as we stress, or perhaps even require, *a specific, singular and personal* vocation, we blind ourselves to the possibilities that exist for us. As long as we think we know where we are going, we are unable to stare clear-eyed at the possibilities before us; we keep looking for those that fit our "vocation" and ignore even the best of possibilities that do not.

They search for the work of their hearts, the place where they can apply their energy with the knowledge that of the many possibilities in the universe, this is the one to which they belong.

I would also caution that it is probably a bad idea to think of vocation in terms of a *permanent* occupation, and that those who pursue such a thing are probably headed for disappointment. As attractive as the idea of a *single* "soul" vocation may be, life itself, in its spiritual sense, seems to find its way as much through the breaking down of patterns as in their continuation. Living in harmony with life itself means being willing to find "soul" meaning within sometimes chaotic circumstances. Sometimes we must change even those things that seem unchanging.

This caution is based on personal experience. In the midst of life's happenstance and mystery, I kept looking for a way of permanence, a way of peace, and I thought that if I found my "true" work, I would find that peace. But those times when I thought I had discovered it often led to the most painful work experiences I have ever had. Now, as I look back, I realize that I find the most resonance between myself and my work when I ask the question, "What am I *called* to do *in this situation*?"

As attractive as the idea of a single "soul" vocation may be, life itself, in its spiritual sense, seems to find its way as much through the breaking down of patterns as in their continuation.

One final caution. Sometimes we misinterpret our own destructive desires as a vocation. This is a terrible problem for us North Americans, as given as we are to making decisions based on our surface perceptions and feelings. I like to think of our consciousness as a chattering monkey riding on the back of a silent gorilla. What we *think* and what we *are* can be very different. The monkey must attend very closely to where the gorilla is headed if it is to find its vocation. This is not easy if the concerns of the gorilla relate to inner pains and difficulties. One of my staff once confessed to me his own sense of vocation. It deeply troubled me because his self-perceived vocation seemed to allow him to cover up serious personal issues. I thought his "sense" of vocation was his way of hiding from who he was, not a foundation for a life of soul work. Facile conclusions about vocation – that is, when we take a point of view of our purpose in life that is not anchored in clear perceptions of who we are – will almost certainly lead us in the wrong direction. The fact it is very difficult to attain a clear perception of who we are just reinforces this caution. The journey to a vocation is fraught with dangers.

Yet for all of that, the concept of vocation has many strengths. Vocation is a powerful way of expressing and feeling our unique abilities as individuals to do specific kinds of work. Our particular collection of experience, skills, and training, combined with the specifics of our personalities, physical makeup, and psycho-social-spiritual being, make us unique in terms of the work we are best-equipped to do. While there is no requirement that our job reflect our uniqueness, and for many of us it does not, when it *does* there is something especially satisfying about it. Each of us is on a soul journey and at times the bending of the path brings us to a stretch where the pieces come together in harmony. Further bends may take us away from that point, but for some time, perhaps months, perhaps years, who we are and what we do come together in a way that reflects our unique capacity. These are certainly times of vocation.

Vocation also helps us understand another similar experience: those times in the midst of our day-to-day workplace activity when we find ourselves *resonating* with our job and we *know* that, in that particular space-time, the work "belongs" to us. Something about the way we are doing the work, the skills we apply, the specific energy or imagination or the intention or resources we use speak of our character, beliefs, and values in such a way that we feel a strong sense of ownership. Something about who we are and that moment of work come together, with an almost transcendent sense of power. The experience may be temporary but we know, about a specific accomplishment, that it was *our* work and that we have done it unusually well; it was *good* work, our soul work. Doing this work is our *calling*, and when we do it we experience our *vocation*.

Finally, I want to note that the way of the master leads far more easily to the experience of vocation than does the way of the savior. Those who reach a point of harmony within the flow know it through the peace they experience. While they may not have found their vocation, in the sense of ultimate belonging, they continually and automatically seek those points where things come together in peace. For those pursuing the way of the savior – the way of risk, of trying new things, of running counter to the flow (if necessary) – the sense of vocation often comes only in retrospect. A sense of harmony is not necessarily something they experience along the way. But saviors look back, sometimes over a vista of many years, and say, "I did that, and I can see that it was right!" In this sense, the journey of the savior can be very lonely, especially at those points when he or she most forcefully opposes the flow of events and therefore may feel most distant from a sense of accomplishment. However, in the long run, the way of the savior is no less full of satisfaction than that of the master. Well done, they can both represent soul work.

The question now is: Where do we start? How do we find this kind of work?

Something about who we are and that moment of work come together, with an almost transcendent sense of power. The experience may be temporary but we know, about a specific accomplishment, that it was our work and that we have done it unusually well; it was good work, our soul work. Doing this work is our calling, and when we do it we experience our vocation.

5

Awakenings

Career Direction for the Soul

Finding our vocation is no easy task. When I was in high school, I had the inevitable chat with the guidance counselor about my future. I sat there, 16, gangly and naive, and told him I was interested in architecture.

"Why do you want to do that?" he asked me in tone I interpreted as negative. He continued, "Have you done any research? Do you know what's involved?" Good questions, sort of. Unfortunately, I had no answers; I did not know what research would be appropriate, let alone what architects actually did. So I sat there. I cannot remember how our interview ended, but I am sure the counselor thought he was wasting his time. For my part, I left his office with the conclusion that architecture was a bad idea. I did not know what I wanted, and beyond some vague idea that designing buildings would be a good thing, I had no idea what I should do.

For many of us it is a powerful time of taking stock of who we are and what we have to offer to the world.

Years later, I discovered that architecture might have been a good option to pursue. I have a lot of design ability, a good head for math and engineering, and a love of human structures. I am also highly creative. Whether I would actually have *become* a good architect is another question, and one that will (almost certainly) remain unanswered.

"What do I want out of life?" and "What do I have to give to life?"

What the situation with the counselor illustrates is both the enormity of the questions confronting anyone facing a career shift (whether at mid-life or just starting out), and the difficulty of knowing how to approach these questions as searchers.

But while this critical decision is so difficult (whether at mid-life or just starting out), it is also a very precious point. For many of us it is a powerful time of taking stock of who we are and what we have to offer to the world. And for a few of us it is a period of insight, where we begin to see within our existence the point of it all. Setting a career direction or making a career shift is one of those important times when all of our core issues are placed in front of us for examination and change. It is one of the few points in our lives when we, ourselves, are our work. (Some of the other times when we do this work relate to other major life transitions, such as the death of a parent, commitment to a life partner, or the birth of a child.)

The questions each of us faces at these points are, "What do I want out of life?" and "What do I have to give to life?" These two questions take us on a journey to the core of our existence. How we answer them with regard to our careers will make a tremendous difference in how we come to and leave the world. This is profound *soul work*.

It is important here not confuse our soul work with a job. As I have repeatedly noted, jobs are transient and the world chaotic. Career-directed soul work is something we are likely to engage in only intermittently, at a number of points throughout our life, as a result of repeatedly taking stock of who we have become and what we have to offer. But what we *can* do, at *every* point, is work to create a more certain and vibrant harmony between who we are and the world we are making. Our souls can be happy in many types of work and perhaps an infinite number of jobs. The questions relate more to *who* we are and *how* we are, than to what we *do*.

Currently in North America, the person beginning a career search faces the daunting reality that there are over 20,000 occupations to consider, each with its own requirements and opportunities, and that more occupations are created each day as new technologies and the realities created by our changing planet coalesce to create new types of work. This vast and changing array should not be viewed as a problem, however, but as an opportunity to find a specific and enjoyable place of engagement. It also means, for a few of us, that our work will itself create new possibilities for others.

Yet it is by overcoming obstacles that we become people of depth and solidity. The challenge facing us is to learn *from them, so that they become an additional resource as we continue to engage the world.*

The world of work is a vast field of opportunity, where you enter with your skills as resources, and where your imagination and intention play a critical role in shaping your pathway through it. This can be a difficult thing to believe when some of those so-called opportunities lead to frustration and a sense of failure, or even to the deep pain of job loss. Yet it is by overcoming obstacles that we become people of depth and solidity. The challenge facing us is to *learn* from them, so that they become an additional resource as we continue to engage the world.

Because I use my model of work as a guide to career planning for the *soul,* you will find that I include more material on your inner state than is typical in most career assist material. In particular, I seek to draw attention to the imagination and intention we bring to this aspect of our existence. As you will recall from earlier chapters, in our work we play out many of the deep concerns of our lives, so we must carefully attend to these issues as we look for new work opportunities. What follows, therefore, is not really a "how to" manual for job seekers, although it contains some of the same material found in other books on the subject. Instead, I seek to provide a new perspective on that material and to add components that are often neglected.

CAREER-PLANNING BASICS

Abilities

When I think about what happened those many years ago in the guidance counselor's office, I realize my real problem at the time was not even the one I thought I had. I wanted more than anything to know what I *should* be doing, to find my one soul work, my specific vocation, and I wanted that counselor to help me. Unfortunately, as is so often the case with spiritual tasks, I was not asking the right question. What I should have been asking at that point was what I *could* do. While it may seem strange to consider *coulds* instead of *shoulds* as the starting point, all career work starts with very practical considerations. There is no point in talking about the *should* if the *could* is outside of your range.

What we *should* do, our soul work, is something contained within the range of what we *can now do,* or *could do* with more training and experience. While I have found people who were determined to do what was obviously impossible for them to do (more on them later), I am convinced that *we are never genuinely called to do that which we cannot do.* The place to start, then, is with our abilities, with what we *can* do.

The list of things we can do includes that enormous range of *abilities, training,* and *experience* we possess. It is not, as some think, made up of a collection of past job descriptions. Each of us has a huge range of things we can actually or potentially do, and only a few of them may ever have been part of our job description.

Let's look at abilities. Each of us has certain innate and biological capabilities. These both limit us and open up possibilities to us. I am severely short-sighted and slightly asthmatic. These limit some of the things I can do. I am highly creative. This expands what I can do. I have also learned how to do many things: write well, talk to groups, plan processes, research, organize groups, and so on. Altogether, this collection of physical and psychological characteristics, combined with skills I have learned, represents my abilities. Each of us has a unique range and selection of abilities. I may be able to do what you cannot, and vice versa. For most of us, our abilities are numbered in the thousands.

In part, we identify our abilities from the names other people give them and the contexts we are used to using them in.

In part, we identify our abilities from the names other people give them and the contexts we are used to using them in. I may think of my abilities as those of a junior soccer coach, for example, when it might be more accurate to say I have the ability to motivate, instruct, organize, and strategize, particularly with children. All too often, however, our abilities are a mystery to us. We never have an opportunity to explore many of our capabilities in order to turn them into abilities, and we may even be only partially aware of the abilities we have developed. This is one of the reasons nearly every job or career transition book has a section on naming abilities, which usually includes a list of hundreds of potential abilities.

Then, of course, we must assess the relative *strength* of our abilities. While many of us have the ability to write, and nearly all of us have the ability to speak, few of us know how to write well and some of us are not able to speak well. The same is true for most other abilities. While we may be *able,* we may not be particularly *well able,* and this means that even when abilities go by the same name, they are not really the same. While it is important for a parent to be able to diagnose and respond to the difference between a low and a high fever, this does not mean that they can realistically list medical diagnosis as an ability. We would expect a much higher level of competence in one who claimed that ability. So in listing our abilities it is important to be honest in rating how they compare to the abilities of others. We need also to recognize that each of us has the potential to develop more abilities or greater skill in the ones we already possess. What we can do now need not be the same as what we can do six months or a year from now.

One of the hardest parts of a career counselor's life is dealing with people who have no clue about the importance of ability. These are the people who strongly believe that they should be doing something that they obviously cannot do. They are also an employer's nightmare. I have counseled such people and, on occasion, I have hired such people. They have their eyes set on a destination they cannot achieve and are all too often convinced that this inability is your fault. For most of us, finding our soul work is a long and sometimes painful task, and being honest about our limits is one of the vital steps we must take.

Interests

Our *interests* are another good indicator of where to look for our soul work. What do we do when we have time, energy, and resources to ourselves? Do we sit in a rocking chair and gaze at the sunset? Or do we join a sports team? Do we draw up plans for home renovations, or work in the garden? What do we do when we are free to choose? If we follow our interests, we know that regardless of where we go, we are aimed in roughly the right direction.

If, as I believe, we need the various parts of our lives to fit together, then we are constantly unconsciously scanning the world around us with a built-in radar. Whenever we find something close to our soul, in this case our soul work, our inner radar says "Ah ha!"

and tells us to get a little closer. This does not mean that the path to our soul work will be a straight line. Often, our path meanders as we confront the demands of our inner lives and as we react to the events life throws our way. Our interests *now* may not be our interests when we find our new work; they may not even be *good* interests, but I am certain they are crucial to our journey.

If that counselor had asked me what I was interested in back in high school, I might have answered two things: reading and building model cars, neither of which was terribly unusual for a boy of 16 who had not yet really discovered girls. If he had pushed further, he would have found that my favorite reading was science fiction, and of science fiction my favorite was the technical kind built on scientific and technical fact. If he had had an opportunity to examine my model cars, he would have discovered that I did a lot of research into what tiny bits and details went where. I had even taken automotives at school in order to improve my knowledge. In short, the counselor would immediately have seen that technical things interested me.

Often, our path meanders as we confront the demands of our inner lives and as we react to the events life throws our way.

Logical career suggestions he could then have made may have included something in the sciences, or technical or engineering careers – even architecture! (These would also have been in keeping with my courses in high school; I took as many sciences as possible and got kicked out of English.) He could have explained the various types of jobs and employment these fields offered and have asked if any of them appealed to me. This approach would have built upon my interests and encouraged me to move toward an area that clearly attracted me.

Searching out interests and following these is not just a method for high school students. In fact, it works better for adults changing careers. As adults, we know a lot more about what we enjoy doing. Life throws a variety of experiences at us and we end up discovering interests we did not know we possessed. Scanning a university calendar one day I discovered a subject called sociology. It intrigued me and I took a course. I took another, and another. Then I looked for similar courses: anthropology, psychology, then geography and history. I dropped computer science. I stopped taking math. New experiences showed me that I was "really" interested in subjects and possibilities far different than what I had assumed when I started. I never did finish an engineering program; instead I graduated with a major in sociology and a minor in psychology. Similarly, later in life, I found myself drifting into the field of church studies and then history, purely following my interests.

Whenever I have changed careers, which I have done a number of times, I have always begun by looking at what I found most interesting in my previous job. Once, the most interesting part of my job related to administrative tasks. Recognizing this led me to a rewarding social services administrative position with a global relief and development organization. Later, when I decided to leave that position, I realized that I enjoyed the problem-solving aspects of my position the most and, on that basis, moved into organizational development and consulting. Consulting led me to uncover a deep love of teaching and subsequently to another career shift. Today you are most likely to find me in front of a class of undergraduates exploring some aspect of history or critical thinking – something I never would have considered years before.

Along the way, I discovered that I loved writing and so I started freelancing the occasional article. Public speaking attracted me, too, so I started putting together presentations on various topics and then, once I saw the need, a whole series on social services management. From interest to interest to interest, I have made my way.

Our lives are not likely to produce a simple, linear career track. Instead, we are likely to move from one place or job to another continually asking the question, *"What am I called to do here and now?"* Our interests are a very powerful reflection of the basic patterns of our lives. They reflect our emotional, psychological, and physical makeup. Once we set ourselves free to follow them, they will steer us a course through the huge range of things we can do and the huge range of things there are available to do. Once we are on track with our interests, our work becomes interesting, motivating, and satisfying. Following our interests will not lead us directly to our soul work, but it will usually draw us close and keep us motivated for the journey.

They have more energy, more joy, and more love for the work they are doing when they see that it reflects their deepest values.

Finally, it's worth noting that had the guidance counselor asked me, as a gawky 16-year-old, if I wanted to teach history to undergraduates, I would have thought he was crazy. Teaching was the last thing on my mind. It took many years of experience for this love to be awakened within me. I became a different person through my life experience and therefore my soul work changed.

DEEP VALUES

One of my greatest personal satisfactions has been to engage myself wholeheartedly in my work because I know that the outcome of my efforts will meet my deepest hopes. I teach history, for example, because I believe that understanding our past can open up our future. I deeply desire that my students gain new eyes with which to see the world, so that they can begin to take on for themselves the responsibility of creating a new and better future. I find deep satisfaction in my work because I know that every word I speak resonates with what I believe is truly important for people. The same is true for those I meet who do work they believe in. They have more energy, more joy, and more love for the work they are doing when they see that it reflects their deepest values.

We must become wise to our values and see them as a key to our soul work. Channeling our career along the lines of our values will bring us more satisfaction than any of the other career "markers," such as wealth or status or power. In fact, we will become more like "saints" in our work – selfless, hard working, compassionate, dedicated, and contributing. We will also know when our investments and the risks we take on fit with who we are. When we are wise to our values and work with them, we begin to build the type of world in which we want to live.

Deep values are something we carry as part of who we are; they change only rarely and with difficulty.

Before proceeding, however, I need to point out that not all values are the same. The most important values are those which I call "deep values," and I will deal with them next. But there are also other values, which I call "preferences." When most career direction handbooks talk about values, what they are really talking about is *preferences.* The difference between these two is important. Deep values tend to be imbedded in our psycho-social-biological make-up. They are the result of early experiences and the outcome of our developmental process. Deep values are something we carry as part of who we are; they change only rarely and with difficulty. Preferences, on the other hand, while they may be powerful, can change or be overruled without a great deal of effort. While it is helpful to know about our preferences, they do not make or break the pursuit of our soul work.

Maintenance

I believe that all of us share at least three deep values, which influence our career choices. First, we value our lives immensely and are willing to work extremely hard to *maintain* our physical, social, psychological, and spiritual well-being. This is one of the key reasons we work, for if we did not value our lives we would give up whenever we met sustained adversity. Throughout much of human history, this value has been seen as the *only* reason for work, and has also been one of the main reasons work gets described as drudgery or toil. We are willing to do all kinds of things to sustain our lives, including things we hate.

This fact brings to light the *negative* influence this value can have on our journey to our soul work. The value we place on maintenance can lead us to accept work that runs against what is otherwise important to us, even when there may be other options. While we must recognize and honor this value, we should not let it determine our lives. That path leads to stagnation, frustration, and spiritual emptiness. On the other hand, when we find and are doing our soul work, we will be energized, even in circumstances that might challenge or threaten our status quo.

The *positive* influence of this value upon us is our drive for self-preservation. Wisdom with this value means knowing how far and how much we can risk before we succumb to anxiety, or worse. It is useful to have a high tolerance for risk if you are a tree-faller, or parachute jumping instructor, or venture capitalist. Others, like myself, are willing to take risks, but in moderation. We are happy to do work that may take us around the globe, or risk our prestige with colleagues, or sacrifice part of our savings to start a new business. Still others have little tolerance for risk. For them, job stability is their number one desire. Respectfully engaged, this value tells us what we *can* do without going too far.

Productive Membership

The second deep value we share is the need to contribute to our collective well-being. While this seems to run counter to the individualistic spirit of our age, with its drive for self-actualization and its worship of the solitary hero, the reality is otherwise. All of us want to contribute positively to our circle of friends, co-workers, and acquaintances. At the core of our being, we want to be productive members of a community that works together. Even self-styled rugged individualists, when pressed, will admit that they do what they do in response to and out of concern for others (and often on the basis of very deep fears).

This is partly why many of us stay with the work we are doing; we have a community where we and our contributions are recognized. The opportunity to be part of such a community of work provides a relief to our spirit. We take more pride in our work and seek the opportunity to be a good member. (Just ask anyone who has been out of work for a while!)

Like most things to do with the soul, this desire is not always a blessing. This value can lead us into dark circumstances when the group we enjoy being part of has goals that are destructive. It can be hard to break free of a work group engaged in destructive activities, if that group is also accepting of us and encouraging of our efforts. I remember my own struggle when faced with a co-worker who was very friendly and supportive of my work in difficult circumstances, but who then wanted me to help him send a highly destructive memo to senior management (actually he wanted me to send it under my name because he thought it would carry more credibility). I refused and the scene in my office when I did so was not pretty. I still regret the loss of my relationship with him. And what, I wonder, would someone have done who needed his approval more than I did?

These negative examples simply indicate how deeply we value this sense of productive cooperation, and how wisely we must respond to it. Rare is the person who can enter a work group saying, "I do not care what they think." Most of us bend very quickly, and woe to us if we do not understand this value and work with it carefully.

As an employer, this value also played a big part in who I hired.

To me, it is more important to find someone who can work with me and the other members of the work team than to find someone with superb skills.

There is a tricky balance to be kept here, because we do not want work teams that dissolve into mushy embraces at every opportunity, or teams that spend all their time supporting one another when there is work to be done. But we also do not want work teams where the members spend more time scrapping than working. I have seen both and neither is good. The best work takes place when people work together respectfully and appreciatively. We need community at work and good places to work have it in healthy doses.

The best work takes place when people work together respectfully and appreciatively.

Reproduction

A third deep value we share is that of reproduction. By this I do not mean biological reproduction, though for many of us it includes that. I am referring to the deep satisfaction we gain when the world looks back at us with our own eyes. Most of us have an intense desire to see ourselves reflected in the world. When the values, interests, commitments, behaviors, styles, and language of those around us are the same as ours, we feel deeply safe. For many of us, this value drives us to reshape the world in our own image, to create an environment that reflects what is inside us, or to find work that will reinforce our image.

Though most of us enjoy stepping out of our world from time to time (isn't that what tourism is all about?) what we really value is *home*, and home is not as much a physical place or a set of relationships as it is an emotional space. Our efforts at reproduction, then, are efforts at creating an atmosphere that is comforting to us (and not necessarily to anyone else) and secure. We seek and rearrange relationships and items in the world around us in order to create circumstances that reproduce the image of home that lies inside our heads. Depending on the intensity of this value, our efforts in this direction can become desperate. There are those who will not travel to another country unless they know that they will be able to find their favorite chain restaurants. There are those who become upset when their co-workers do not tell them what they want to hear, or act and or look the way they desire.

Personally, I enjoy chaos. To me, chaos speaks of creativity and opportunity, and these things are part of my sense of "home." As a boss, I build a working environment that is somewhat chaotic. Roles are never completely straightforward, tasks are always somewhat ambiguous, and it is often difficult to say when things are done. These are the things I enjoy seeing; they reflect what is inside my head and I gain tremendous satisfaction from seeing them come to life in the world around me. On the other hand, I have told the story of working in a stringently ordered environment. While my colleagues seemed to motor along quite well, I found the policy book destructively confining. I finally quit. Not only could I not remake the work in my image, its structure ran deeply contrary to my image of what I want the world to be like.

Again, this value tends to be disregarded in most of the career material. We rarely recognize in our guidance practices how deeply this value affects us. This may be because those of us of Western European extraction (at whom most career guidance material is aimed) share a profoundly similar sense of how the world looks. Our workplace reproductive urges tend, just like our children, to reflect our white skin. However, this overlooks the diversity we genuinely experience, and which our increasingly multicultural world is forcing onto us. It is far easier to find culturally intolerable working arrangements now than it was not many years ago. We need, in ways almost beyond imagining, to see the world in our own image, and wisdom requires that we take this into account. We may or may not find such an environment and it may or may not be a good thing. But in every case, the value we place on re-production is something we need to be very aware of.

Other Deep Values

Besides these three deep values, which I believe we all share, there are also those deep values that are unique to each one of us and that are discovered either in flashes of insight or through long living. These values are the result of the accumulated experiences of our lives and the shape of our souls and they are never the same from one person to another. One of my own, particular deep values is my desire that the world make sense. I know other people for whom child safety represents a deep value.

Those values which may be peculiar to us may take longer to understand, but by following our interests we will come close.

Regardless of what our deep values are, it is essential that we discover them, for if we do not, *they* will discover us, usually in painful ways. We violate our deep values only at great cost and we rarely do so, except when we find a conflict between them (such as when the value we place on productive membership clashes with the value we place on reproduction). Wisdom requires that we treat these values as givens and seek work and life options that allow us to engage them fully and in life-giving ways. Our failure to do so will haunt us.

It is not always an easy task to discover or map our deep values. While I valued a sensible universe long before I sat in that high school guidance counselor's office, more than ten years would pass before I began to gain a sense of it, and nearly 20 years would pass before I could put words to it. The good news is that at least three of these deep values are relatively common and we only need to pay attention to how they have expressed themselves in our lives. Those values which may be peculiar to us may take longer to understand, but by following our interests we will come close. And, as we note which things help us to feel satisfied, we will be directed to them. How we respond to suffering or to strong obstacles in our lives will also point the way to our deep values.

Preferences

Preferences are the kind of values that occasionally show up in career search materials. They are most commonly presented as a paired list: do you value this or that? Do you value creativity or do you value established routine? Do you prefer to work alone or do you prefer to work with others? While these preferences are interesting and sometimes helpful when evaluating a specific type of work, most of them will bend

No matter how much we are paid, if our core values are not being met then we are likely to see ourselves as underpaid.

or change considerably in light of our deep values and I do not believe we need to worry too much about them. Once we know and are working with our deep values, these secondary values or preferences will arrange themselves to fit.

One of the best examples of this phenomenon is the value we place on money. Many career direction books ask us to rate (among other things) how important money is to us and then, on that basis, evaluate particular career options. For example, pursuing a career in child care is not a good idea if making lots of money is something you value highly; childcare workers are generally among the most poorly paid workers. But my experience is that we value money the most when our deep values are not being met. If our deep values are met while we are making the wages of a childcare worker, then I suspect we will be happy with our work, regardless of what we might have thought about the importance of money beforehand. Conversely, no matter how much we are paid, if our core values are not being met then we are likely to see ourselves as underpaid.

EXPERIENCE

So far, we have discussed abilities, interests, and values. Each of these represents an important component of finding our soul work. Finally, I think we need to look at what we have already done, our experience. While what we have done is no sure sign of what we *can* do, or what we *should* do, it is a good indication – sometimes positive, sometimes negative – of both.

Particularly as we get older, we often find ourselves returning to the same activities. These activities represent an important marker in terms of our experience. If that guidance counselor had asked me what I kept coming back to – in other words, what I had experience doing – he would have discovered that what I had done was build houses. This was a requirement of growing up in the family home. Dad built a new house every year or two and we kids were required to participate. It was how we earned summer income, but more than that, it was a part of family life. So very early I learned to work with cement, hammer a nail properly, lay out a wall, and put up the wallboard. With that small bit of information that counselor could have both gained a tremendous insight into why I considered architecture, and into what I could do. Then he could have asked, "Did you enjoy it?" and, if I had been honest, I would have said, "No, I hated it." That would have been a good caution around the architecture and perhaps have opened the door to a larger conversation about what kinds of things I had done which I *did* enjoy.

It does not take too many years of activity – at home, at school, in the community, or in the workplace – to establish very important patterns. Imagine someone who has operated a dry-cleaning business, managed a ball team, taken regular vacations with his family, and attended church every Sunday. In this imaginary person we see energy around the poles of family, community, stability, and spirituality. If he were to consider making a career shift, it is unlikely that he should take up work on an off shore oil rig. More appropriate alternatives might include the operation of a sporting goods store, or perhaps a religious goods store. Or consider someone who "temps" as an administrative assistant, does a lot of free lance graphic design, has maintained no long-term relationships, and enjoys mountain biking. In this person, energy is transient, perhaps highly creative, and tied to nature. For her, career alternatives are unlikely to involve a long-term job and a life in the suburbs. Alternatives might relate to environmental initiatives or multi-media work.

In each case, what we have done provides important clues to what we should do next.

COMMUNITY

While in today's world careers are seen as the prerogative and concern of the individual, this overlooks one of the most important aspects of career transitions – the field of opportunity within which we function. We think about change in the context of other people and we come to our life decisions in the context of other people. What we do not normally think about is how those people affect both our experience and our opportunities. Yet what we *have done* and what we *will do* in our lives are things that emerge, in large measure, as a result of the beliefs, perspectives, responses, and support of those around us.

As I reflect on my own journey, I know that genuine progress has always taken place in the context of a supportive community. Sometimes that community was invisible to me at the time, but looking back I can see it clearly. All of us make our way in a context that includes other people. At a very practical level, this can translate into financial support during a difficult time of transition. At a theoretical level, how we come to see ourselves and our soul journey is based in part on the way we encounter others on the journey. Always, there are people present, helping us along.

If, as is often the case in our transient society, you do not currently have a community of companions, I am aware of at least three ways to find one. The first and most obvious way is to intentionally join an already existing community, such as a church or religious community, a service club, or some other neighborhood association. The second way is through service. By serving in some capacity, by working to improve the situation of others, by giving some of what you have, you take a significant step toward community. The third way involves vulnerability. Open yourself to others, become honest with them, reveal your weak points and your hurts. Once again, self-help or religious groups can be a *safe* place to try these latter two suggestions, but *any* community group, collective organization, or community initiative can provide the context.

By serving in some capacity, by working to improve the situation of others, by giving some of what you have, you take a significant step toward community.

Mentors

Mentors are a special part of any community. Someone who takes a special interest in our journey and who can guide us is a tremendous gift. A number of people have been mentors to me. What strikes me about each is that they could see more potential in me than I could see in myself. Two of them were considerably older than I was and perhaps this says something about what we need in a mentor. Perhaps we need someone who, as a result of their maturity and experience, can steer us in directions we have trouble understanding. But once, a student of mine became my mentor. At a difficult point in my life, this person helped me to see the "thing" inside myself that would lead to the next step. So in one sense, almost anyone can be a mentor. The essential quality for a mentor is that they must be able to see, accurately, something of who you are and where you need to go.

When we are young, mentors are especially important. As we take our initial steps into maturity, the wise guidance of a mentor can make all the difference: the difference between clarity and confidence on the one hand, and confusion and fear on the other. A mentor can point out to us the logical connections between who we are and what we are experiencing. A mentor can help us to overcome perceptual barriers and can show us the strengths we possess and could use in our particular circumstance. Sometimes mentors can intervene or assist in situations directly, though this is rare.

Mentors are not nearly as scarce in reality as they often seem. I suspect that there are more wise people willing to offer help than there are those willing to be helped. Perhaps this is due, once again, to the myth that we must make it on our own. Or perhaps we need training in order to see and use mentors. Regardless, they are rarely more than a request for advice away.

Networks

Networks, those sometimes diffuse strands of connection we make with people around us, are another important aspect or feature of community. It has become a truism that we are never more than six levels of connection away from everyone else on the planet, but this overlooks something more important about our networks. Our networks shape who we are and are directly responsible for the opportunities we encounter.

Typically, we think of ourselves as individuals who connect to other folk in more and less direct ways, which end the moment we stop the interaction. What we usually overlook is that in each connection we give something of ourselves and gain something of the "other," and this has a lasting impact. The pleasantries of day-to-day interaction are culturally standard ways of ensuring that our connections build us up through positive experience.

We appreciate ourselves more in the company of those who are pleasant. In fact, we (usually) become more pleasant as the folk with whom we connect are pleasant to us. The smiling clerk at the store, with whom we may interact for only a few seconds, is a moral force for good in our lives (even if they are struggling to be pleasant). That clerk, through their pleasantness, supports and affirms us in our positive self-regard and our own pleasantness.

While this transformative power is real at the level of day-to-day trivial interactions, it is even more real at the intimate level of the relationship we have with our family and friends, or with the people we interact with at and through our work. In each of those interactions, too, we give something of ourselves and receive something of the other person or persons. What we give and what we gain ranges from feelings to practical skills to perceptions. Especially when we are younger, what we gain can be profoundly transformative. We may become different people, with different desires, perceptions, and abilities, based on how those around us relate to us. And as we age, what we give becomes more transformative for others.

This means that as we explore new career possibilities, the people we relate to will shape the opportunities and potentials we see. A group of "young buck" sales reps will push us to see the opportunities and potential in sales (and will give us effective strategies and guide us there). A group of disciplined senior nurses will push us to see the opportunities and potential in nursing (and will give us effective strategies and guide us there). Our current relational networks give us the eyes to see and the ability to respond effectively.

Implied in what I've said above is the fact that our relational networks will point us in directions they are comfortable with. They will encourage us to go places they see as good – good (perhaps) for us, but certainly good in terms of their own perspective on the world. They will give us names, introduce us to others, and tell us how to respond effectively to those we meet along whatever path they recommend. Conversely, they will resist any effort on our part to move in a direction they do not see as good.

Who we *are* and who we are *becoming* are functions of our networks. The people with whom we interact represent our connections with the world, and our guides to effective existence in the world. Well-chosen and soul-directed, they will instill in us a more positive view of ourselves and help us to become people who can give more to the good inherent in the universe itself. A good network can, if we will allow it, make us good.

In this light, I caution that networks do not exist to be exploited. Many in the business and career-counseling community view networks as simply another kind of resource. While networks *can* be a resource, they are much more than that. In some respects, our networks are what make us human. For that reason, they are sacred and need and deserve nurture and protection. We must always honor the sacredness of each person in our network. While we may change our path and change our networks, we must do so in ways that leave a lasting positive impact. Yes, these people may be the key to a better future, but along the way – in the moment of interaction – they need to experience *us* as a key to *their* better future. Our future as individuals depends on our future as relational communities.

NEXT STEPS

Often, the hardest part of making a transition is getting started. In the first appendix, I work through eight steps that can help you get going.

Talking

However, the key is to start talking. Talking is the first step to exploring our soul and the first step to changing our circumstances. Talking is the first part of that work. (And I am aware that for some personalities, talk itself is work!)

There are four things that make talk so powerful as a next step. The first is that talking to others is an important way of listening to ourselves. As we speak, we weigh the truth of our words against our actual situation. All of us know that feeling – that self-confirmation that this thing I am saying is true (or false). If there is a strong dissonance between our words and our experience, we will know it; major self-truths cannot be suppressed. Therefore, we can, by speaking, come to genuinely understand our situation and begin to explore our options.

While networks can be a resource, they are much more than that. In some respects, our networks are what make us human. For that reason, they are sacred and need and deserve nurture and protection.

The second thing that makes talking so powerful is that it represents a way of personal transformation. Inside each of us exists an often-conflicted collection of dreams, hopes, perceptions, and fears. How we bring order to the chaos inside us is up to us, but talking is one of the most powerful methods we have at our disposal. As we express what's inside us, the balance between the parts shifts: the fear becomes unreasonable (or reasonable), the dream becomes reasonable (or unreasonable). As we talk about what's important to us, we bring order to the chaos and we change who we are.

The third thing about talking is that it opens us to dialogue with others. We are surrounded by people who have ideas about our capabilities. Sometimes they are only waiting for an opportunity to let us know. If they happen to be well-placed in a field in which we are interested, they can provide invaluable feedback about our future prospects. This does mean, of course, that we have to listen as well as talk. It may also mean asking questions and preparing them in advance.

The fourth thing that makes talking so powerful is that it can itself create opportunities. The world is neither static nor stable. Talking is an expression of personal power and, as such, changes our relationships with those around us. We begin to create the environment around us, and that means that others start to adjust to us. All of this takes place on the basis of the content of our conversations. When we talk about work opportunities, or career direction, people begin to rethink who we are in relation to them, and then act to provide opportunities (or sometimes to resist our efforts). Once a few people start responding, we have no idea how far that transformation may extend. The whole world may change for us!

Once a few people start responding, we have no idea how far that transformation may extend. The whole world may change for us!

Finally, through our talking, we will form or expand our community of support – that critically important field of opportunity that makes our journey easier. Talking is one way to invite others into our lives and to make genuine long-term connections.

I remember one young man who came into my office years ago seeking advice on his next career step. His wife had been transferred to the community and he was at loose ends. He told me about his training and about his hopes for the future. While he was talking, I realized that he had a set of skills I had been looking for so, very shortly thereafter, I offered him a job. He stalled at first (the offer was far outside of his training), but finally accepted the position. He did an excellent job and I was extremely happy I had hired him. Eventually, he left to take another position, but I have kept in touch with him. In fact, I had lunch with him recently. As we discussed his current job, I realized that despite many external differences, he is still doing the work I had given him, and is still enjoying it tremendously. One conversation can change your life.

6

Perspective

Compassionate Engagement

A friend of mine is a business owner who once reflected on the progress of his business. He told me that he could still remember the day he signed his first contract for more than $100,000. It seemed absolutely momentous to him and worth every effort to achieve it. He put in long hours to make it happen. Then he told me about his most recent contract worth $6 million. He put in long hours to make that happen, too: long hours and a commitment to the 60 jobs on the line and the long-term worth of the company. He mused, "Now I hardly look at anything under $500,000. It doesn't seem worth the effort. Sometimes I wonder what will be worth the effort after I sign a $10 million contract, or a $20 million contract?"

These folks are all engaged in their work, and often very successfully. But it is an engagement that comes with a very high cost and it is an engagement that does not accurately place us in our world.

Then he talked about how he gets so caught up in each new achievement and how after he makes the deal nothing has *really* changed. He still has the same longings, the same quest to see what lies around the next business corner. In fact, in some parts of his life, things may have become worse. A big contract can take him three months of 60- to 70-hour weeks to set up, weeks that leave him completely exhausted. Yet at the end of it, once he has the deal, he recognizes that he has almost missed everything that has happened in his family or the world around him for those three months. He says that at that point he needs to spend time carefully with his partner and children so that he can re-establish his ties with them.

My friend is more honest than many. The social worker who takes calls every weekend from clients, the teacher who spends evenings and weekends grading papers, the many who spend far too much time with their (important) work and too little time with their families and communities are all too common. These folks are all engaged in their work, and often very successfully. But it is an engagement that comes with a very high cost and it is an engagement that does not accurately place us in our world.

The engagement these people are undertaking represents one part of what it means to work: we are engaged in transforming the world. It is a powerful thing to do and it can mean much to ourselves and those around us. Often this engagement is highly rewarded. Sometimes, it seems as if our whole culture conspires to reward this over-focus on work, this passionate engagement with what we are doing.

My challenge to my friend and to all those who engage their work in this way is to ensure that this is not the *only* way you act in the world. Especially do not act as if your passionate engagement with your work is the *only* way to be in the world. There is another side to existence that must be honored and that is *compassion*, the *suffering with*.

But this is the temptation: having become regarded as success-ful through engagement, it is extremely difficult to recognize that simple compassion is also required – no less so than the engagement – if our full work, our *life work* is to succeed.

The thing about work and about our lives is that they are chaotic. We may experience a long period of stasis, followed by wild change; or we may engage in a long period of sustained, high-energy work, and then find ourselves in a lull. No matter how carefully we plan, both will be part of our lives. Our tendency, based on our past successes and preferred approach to life, is to see the wild changes as either a chance to finally get on with things, or a temporary time of decision making in a long-term movement with the flow. Or to say it another way, we may see the high-energy work as our way to get to the real lull that we are searching for, or we may find the lull to be an unwelcome break in the high-energy work we live for. But no matter which way we come at it, our tendency is to overlook that both sides are always present and that neither is a break from nor preparation for the other. Chaos is the rule and we must be able to flex with whatever comes our way. We must find a place of *compassionate engagement* – a place of commitment to change that can suffer with, and a place of suffering with that is happy to see change.

The thing about work and about our lives is that they are chaotic.

This is not, I caution, about finding balance. I do not believe in balance. I do not think life offers us balance. My experience is that life always offers us too much or not enough of what we are looking for and that we are always lurching from one side to the other, desperately hoping we do not fall over the edge. There is no middle. Because I believe the universe itself is a dance of chance and necessity, there cannot be a middle. We are not meant to be at peace.

We are meant, however, to *pursue* peace. Our job is to foster a character that knows its direction in the midst of the chaos. That character is one that knows both compassion and engagement, and that takes up both as necessary, to the best of its ability, and to the maximum of its understanding. We cannot control our world. At times we must resist our world. In our efforts at either, we can only succeed from time to time. But we can always seek peace. We do that through the perspective we take to our existence, the perspective of compassionate engagement.

That businessman who knows he could work 70-hour weeks, 52 weeks of the year, is an example of compassionate engagement. He has a reputation for running an organization that turns out excellent work and he knows that there is a far larger market for his product than he has tapped to date. But what holds him back is the recognition that to pursue those possibilities, to turn his organization into a $100-million-a-year outfit, would cost, first, his relationships, and then, his health. Currently, he has an informal agreement with his family that he only puts his efforts into one or two major new clients per year. That agreement is not easy for him to live by, but it helps him keep what is genuinely important in mind. Furthermore, he does not try to manage his family as he does his company. He has agreed to bend and flex with them, to follow their needs, to go with their desires. Similarly, he tries, though less successfully, to attend to the rest of the world around him. While its pace is far slower than he is comfortable with, he understands that this, too, is part of the way things are.

The consequence of all this is that he will never make the Fortune 500 with his company, or be recognized as a great business leader. He *will*, however, be remembered by his family. His community will remember his work on various boards and with non-profits. His employees will remember him as a man who modeled both good work and a good life. These achievements are perhaps not what they *could* be, not the type that will get him untold wealth or media recognition, but they are what they *should* be. While I would never call him balanced, I would say that he has a strong sense of compassionate engagement.

Imagining Compassionate Engagement

It is not easy to bring together compassion and engagement in our character. As an orientation, it is a shifting point that begins with the recognition that both are essential. Once we recognize that, we are on our own again, struggling to keep our feet and keep moving. But we will pursue peace regardless. In what follows, I work through the meaning of compassionate engagement as it relates to the model of work developed in Chapter 3. Then I look at how it works out in one specific and important life process. But I must admit that what follows tends to be one-sided, as *I* am somewhat one-sided. (Being able to perceive both sides does not mean I am *comfortable* with both sides.)

The essence of compassionate engagement is to focus on process as well as on outcome.

The essence of compassionate engagement is to focus on *process* as well as on *outcome*. Of course, every process is linked to every other process and it gets very hard to know the precise boundaries of each. *Our* work is affected by the work of *others*. What we experience at *work* affects how we feel at *home*, and vice versa. So, too, some work processes run through a number of days or weeks. Other projects or processes will last a few months. Still others will wrap up in a matter of hours. Writing a book, such as this one, may take *years* from conception to completion. In other words, there are many processes and many *types* of processes in our lives, and each one could be the basis for compassionate engagement. So where do we start?

In order to obtain this perspective of compassionate engagement, we first need a new vision of ourselves. And in order to acquire this new vision, we need to introduce a new concept: the frame of reference. This concept comes from the field of social psychology and the pioneering work of Irving Goffman in the 1960s. According to Goffman, we carry many frames of reference inside our heads, complex conceptual structures that tell us how we should behave in particular circumstances. Typically, we deal with day-to-day life by subconsciously "flipping" through these frames until we find the one(s) we think apply.

For example, when I go into a workplace as a consultant, I "flip" on my work character. I am not always proud of that character – tough, clear, to the point, independent, suspicious, and less-than-happy about the unknown compromises I may be required to make. It is kind of a "cowboy" mentality that I "put on." This man (is it truly me?) is capable of doing a tremendous amount of work under sometimes arduous conditions and of getting quickly to the core of problems. But what he is not always good at is listening to feelings, or developing relationships with people, or dealing with the corporate politics.

By changing or modifying these frames of reference, or by adding new ones, we begin to change the way we operate day to day.

By changing or modifying these frames of reference, or by adding new ones, we begin to change the way we operate day to day. In my case, if I could "flip" on a different work character, I would act differently on the job.

This is exactly what compassionate engagement means. If I take compassionate engagement seriously, then I must change or modify my frame of reference in order to bring a more appropriate "persona" into being. In my case, I need to begin to imagine myself as one who can not only engage (I do that well) but also as one who can be compassionate. I need to engage for change, and at the same time respond harmoniously to the forces at work in the setting. If I could "flip" on a "healer," "medicine man," or "guru" work character, I would act differently on the job and perhaps be more effective in some circumstances.

The Hard Work of (re-)Developing Character

Changing our frames of reference is not easy. They are deeply rooted inside us, often locked into place by powerful early memories and experiences. Some are locked into place by the way they help to feed and shelter us, or help to get us sex. Then they are etched deep into our brain through their repeated use. In every case, they point our eyes in certain directions, tell us what to do, and shape our thinking in very specific ways.

In order to change our frames of reference, we must do two things. First, we must imagine new possibilities (the focus of this chapter). Second, we must begin to act differently (something I will leave to you). When new imagination and new actions come together, our old frames of reference begin to break down and we construct new ones. We gain new brains with which to think, new eyes with which to see, new fingers with which to work. The change happens slowly, but it is radical nonetheless.

In order to change our frames of reference, we must do two things. First, we must imagine new possibilities. Second, we must begin to act differently.

Our imaginations get inspired in many ways. One of them is our leisure time. (I'm starting in the easy places). The books we read, the movies we see, the television shows we watch, all feed us with images of people doing things. As I watch the Gilmore Girls deal with the struggles of their lives, and cope more and less well, I gain new perceptions on the world. As I read a biography and see how someone else has responded to the real challenges of their life, I gain new insights into how others have dealt with things that I may face. As I relax with friends and listen to their stories, I gain a new appreciation for people and their possibilities, and therefore for my own possibilities. Each time I undertake any one of these kinds of leisure activities, I change myself a little, become a little more of that of which I am watching, reading, or listening to. My frames of reference shift with every act of leisure imagination.

We can augment this shift by deliberately "trying on" roles. We can imagine how various people would cope with our world, make our decisions, or do our work. This does not mean that, if we do this, we will act the way we imagine they would act. Rather, we are developing new patterns of connection within the brain that expand our capacity to change in our own situation. And sometimes, if the result feels good, we may actually try that behavior.

Trying to model our mentors and the positive examples of those around us is another powerful route into our imaginations. One of my mentors is wonderfully direct, in a way that makes you realize he cares for you. Every time I'm with him, I watch him, listen to the words he chooses, the way he speaks, so that I can learn how to be more like him in my directness. Another acquaintance just made a major shift out of a partnership to working on his own. He is a much gentler person than I am and so I watch to see how he makes his way through the difficulties of business on his own, so that I can teach myself a gentler path through business. This same person also has a highly developed sense of the divine presence in his work and so I listen to his words about how the divine works in and through him, to give me clues to how and where I should look for the divine presence in my own work.

Still, I am careful about who I try to emulate, and about how I emulate them. Not every "saint" is someone I should copy. My personality is my own and it will only bend so far. I have learned, for example, that the boisterously outgoing are not good people for me to try to be like, regardless of how wonderful they may be. I cannot do what they do, no matter how hard I try, and I only become exhausted in the attempt. Instead, I look for people who are at least somewhat like me, so that I already have something familiar upon which to build.

I also attend to the negative in other people's experience. As good as they may appear to me, they, too, have their weaknesses (and they may even be trying to emulate *me*!). Sometimes a mentor's approach does *not* work and at those points I try to understand how I can do something different. One of my very wise teachers was fired from his position. It was a brutal, drawn out event, and I watched how he responded. The experience taught me a lot about what to do, and about what *not* to do, and I have been very clear ever since how I try to be both like and *unlike* him in my own times of difficulty. Then, too, sometimes *we* are the ones who have the best perspective. When I look at how others engage their world, I often see my own strategy being reinforced. Sometimes, *who we are is the best we can be* in that situation, and change would not be a good thing.

While the influence on our imagination of leisure pursuits and the people around us is an important thing to consider and an excellent place to begin the work of changing our frames of reference, it will be even more helpful to review the model of work developed earlier in this book. Doing so will move us into the more difficult task of not only trying to change our frames of reference, but of trying to re-educate ourselves in regard to our sense of work.

When we consider the model of work already developed, with its many parts, it is not hard to recognize that at each step in the process of our work we engage one or more frames of reference. From our initial imagining, to the learning we take from the completed work, specific frames of reference shape what we see, feel, hear, and think. If we realize this, we can examine *which* frames we put on, and how, and can then open ourselves to change.

Let's look at the most important points of interaction between our frames of reference and the work we do: our initial imagining, our intentions, our skills, our efforts, and our learning. While the other parts of the model require frames of reference as well, these five deal with the areas where compassionate engagement can most easily and powerfully be implemented.

Compassionately Engaged Imagination

As I've already argued, all work begins with an act of imagination. *How* we imagine and *what* we imagine play a huge role in determining our future. While we may think of imagination as the random, dreamlike images and thoughts that drift through our mind, we can also focus our minds to select the range and shape of our imagining. It is when we *do* this that we begin to engage our frame of reference. Of course, even at this level, some of our imaginings will merely be deliberate fantasies. Others, however, will be careful examinations of and reflections upon aspects of our world. Yet both the deliberate fantasy and the careful examination represent aspects of our being brought to conscious engagement, through the frame of reference we put on while we are doing the imagining.

For example, when I lie back and put my mind into imagination mode, I have two frames of reference that constantly hover, waiting to be used. One is my "visual" frame; I like to "see" the relationships between color and form. I imagine photographing aspects of my world and trying to select what I see as particular pleasing arrangements. The other frame of reference that is constantly waiting in the wings is my "meaning" frame. In this frame, I ask myself "What is the underlying pattern here?" Or, "What are these people *really* up to?" And I let my mind go. What comes back will reflect these frames. Of course, there are many other frames of reference we can use to shape our imaginings.

Compassionate engagement at the level of our imagining involves sorting our frames of reference, and then choosing those that we know reflect our understanding of the highest "good." While imagining "the highest good" may not sound terribly exciting, it is vital that we do so. What is the best we could be in this situation? What would be a better outcome? What is the positive force underlying what we are perceiving?

It is not necessary to use this frame of reference *all* the time, but by doing so on a regular basis we increase our ability to see new and positive possibilities in the world around us; we begin to rewire our brains with the result that the world actually comes to *look* more positive.

Most of us already do all of this, but we can always do it more. More importantly, we can consciously choose to engage our imaginations in this way at times when it does not feel natural to do so. *Especially* we should do it when it does not feel natural to do so.

Compassionately Engaged Intentions

Our intentions *always* come straight from our frame of reference. Whenever we set out to do a job, it is the job that tells us what we should be trying to do. Our intention to maximize profits, or to sell more aggressively, or to care with appropriate professionalism, to name a few examples, will be a function of our jobs as sales managers or social workers.

Compassionate engagement at the level of our imagining involves sorting our frames of reference, and then choosing those that we know reflect our understanding of the highest "good."

This makes our intentions one of the most crucial points in our move toward compassionate engagement in our work. If our intentional framework is not one that includes "compassionate engagement" then we will not be compassionately engaged. Unfortunately, some employers would not consider compassionate engagement an appropriate frame of reference to use in the workplace. Generally, however, any such absence can be rectified simply by bringing our attention to it.

In my experience, we can take a step back in almost any job and ask ourselves, "What do I intend here?" If I am not compassionate in my intentions, that is, if I have put my sensitivity to others and their needs to one side (perhaps because I believe that this is what the work calls for), I can take a long hard look at myself and my work and ask "Does the work *really* demand this of me?" and "Is this really the *kind* of person I want to be?" and make changes accordingly. If I identify that I am both engaged and compassionate, I can reinforce that set of intentions. But most of us find that we are out of tune on one side or the other; our intentions are rarely appropriately compassionate *and* engaged. And therefore we can change.

The impact of this shift is hard to overstate. Once we decide that we will hold both together, to the best of our ability and understanding, we will immediately find that certain aspects of our work change in regard to their level of importance. We may begin to reflect more on the ethics of specific actions, or work a little harder, or be more pleasant to our co-workers. The possibilities expand like ripples and, under the right conditions, grow in power as they flow out. This is always the case when our "perspective" on our work comes from the soul. Bringing our compassion and our commitment to our intentions makes all the difference in the world. Try it! You'll see!

COMPASSIONATELY ENGAGED EFFORT

Like our intention, our efforts very quickly move to the heart. In every case, our efforts are framed or focused by internal dialogues and experiences that tell us how much of ourselves to apply. If we are not compassionately engaged, our efforts will be wrong: too much, too little, or not sensitive enough. By stepping back that half step that allows us to reflect on our framing, to listen to our inner forms of perception with regard to our efforts, we can see where and how we need to change.

Compassionately Engaged Skill

Every work we undertake requires a set of skills and every skill is a technique for engaging the world and transforming it. It may be the surgeon's skill with a knife, the mechanic's skill with a wrench, or the architect's skill with form and space. All of us have a vast body of skills, which we apply in order to accomplish the changes required by our work. While the specific transformation of the world we undertake may be tiny, it still represents a powerful engagement by us. Understanding how to compassionately engage our skills is thus of utmost importance.

Unlike the previous components of work, most of us use skills at a "tacit" level. This means that we have learned to apply them in such a way that, for the most part, we do not "think" about them. Our skills often exist outside of our consciousness. So while a skill is a tool for engagement, we ourselves are not necessarily "engaged" with the world while we are using them.

For example, when I am in a classroom I rarely consciously ask myself "who here is struggling and needs special attention." I just go into "teacher" mode and unconsciously attend, then adjust what I am saying, sometimes repeating, until the person or people to whom I am "attending" begin to demonstrate signs of comprehension. A skilled mechanic knows without thinking when something is being tightened properly, or lined up correctly. No matter what the profession, occupation, or task, the skilled function outside of consciousness. This means we are in for a very difficult time when we come to think through compassionate engagement of our skills.

My father used to say, "Good-enough is not good enough." He was talking about how an adequate application of skill was not necessarily an appropriate application of skill. Specifically, he wanted me to do a better job of placing boards for a paneled ceiling, which meant matching the grain patterns and not dinging so many boards with misplaced hammer blows. And I did improve. I learned to sense the line of the grain and how it changed the lie of the wood and its aesthetic relationship to the other boards. I learned how to grasp and swing the hammer more effectively. And I became, in the process, more passionately engaged in the work and more sensitive to the relationship others would have with my work. My father would not have said that I was putting my "soul" into my work (that was not the way he thought about things), but, in retrospect, improving my skills and putting my "soul" into my work *were* powerfully interactive forces. Improving my skills was a function of my compassionate engagement, and my compassionate engagement was a function of my skills.

To be truly compassionately engaged, we must be the very best we can be at the work we are doing. We must be prepared to strive for excellence rather than willing to settle for "good enough." The quality of our skills reflects our compassionate engagement. As we learn what "putting our soul into our work" *looks* like, we begin to find within ourselves the engagement that drives the work, and the compassion that is sensitive to its interaction with others.

COMPASSIONATELY ENGAGED LEARNING

As we discovered with compassionately engaged imagination and intentions, what we *learn* from our work and how we learn it grows directly from the frames of reference we begin with. Our work always produces consequences from which we can learn. The only question is, "*What* should we be learning?" Or to put it slightly differently, when we are working, to what should we be attending so that we can become more compassionately engaged?

Phrased in this way, we can see that work and learning operate as a perpetual feedback loop, where our attention to what we are learning changes all future cycles of our work. If I attend to those things that speak of compassion and engagement as I go about my work and observe its outcomes, I will be changed and will grow, becoming both more compassionate and more engaged. In other words, whatever I attend to I become more sensitive to in the future. Compassion and engagement become both the frame of reference for learning, and the "lesson" that I learn, the thing that I begin to embody. The act of attending changes my perspective and changing my perspective changes everything that happens next.

Compassionate Engagement Equals Love

When we reach this point of learning, something else begins to happen as well. Having begun to learn to see compassionate engagement, we find ourselves catching a wave of energy that powerfully enhances our learning, our work, and our life. This is because embracing compassionate engagement represents a shift that changes the way the energy of the universe flows through us. We stand, as I have said, in the midst of forces and energies. Those forces are not neutral. Having come to see the possibilities of a new way of seeing, we are inevitably swept into a new way of being more in harmony with the forces that bring our world into existence.

Having begun to learn to see compassionate engagement, we find ourselves catching a wave of energy that powerfully enhances our learning, our work, and our life.

Through compassionate engagement, we reach a place of *love*. As we bring them together, into every aspect of our work, and as we learn and change day by day, our work becomes an act of love. Compassionately engaged, we move and live into a partnership with the "higher" power of love that drives existence itself. And I know of nothing more powerful, even in the midst of difficult circumstances, than feeling that our work has become *more than our work*. I believe we all want and need to participate in transcendence, to contribute toward the ultimate good of the universe, and in our work it can happen. When it does, we are thrilled to step back from our work; we return from our work thrilled to be home and thrilled to be part of the human community at all levels.

Not only this, our work takes on a new meaning for others, which makes it still greater. When we open ourselves to the transcendent, our creativity is unleashed. We can do new and better things, which the higher powers of existence will work with us to discover. And the ripples will spread out into the lives and souls of those around us.

A Continuing Journey

It should be clear by this point that personal, compassionate engagement with our work is not just a matter of changing our perspective. It is not that we have simply changed our minds and now we are happy. Compassionate engagement involves much *inner* work, the goal of which is to help us live differently in a very real way so that we can do our work as fully human and celebrating beings.

This is not an easy task. There is nothing more difficult than transforming ourselves. We throw up barriers, pretend we have changed when we have not, and generally try to avoid our problems. More often than not, when we make real change it is because we have to, not because we want to.

The good news is that once we start, we cannot turn back – and not just because the rewards are too great. (Indeed, compassionately engaged, our work becomes deeply satisfying.) Rather, once we start, we are transformed into people who are better than we were. We are different forever. There are also very few of us who, once embarked upon compassionate engagement, will not sense the divine presence at our side. When that happens, how can we help but continue?

7

Posture

Critical Openness

One man I know spends his time on the way to work praying. He says he actually enjoys the rush hour. It is a time of meditation and prayer while he drives the familiar route from home to office. Once at his office, he straps on a telephone headset, and from then till he leaves work at the end of the day he is a blur of words, incoming and outgoing, as he brokers cars. He says he used to find his day stressful, but since he started praying his way to work, it has become far easier.

For him, it was the frenzy of his work that forced him to become a more spiritual person and to get the rest of his life together.

I spent a good part of one afternoon interviewing him at work, as the incoming calls interrupted our conversation. I had been told that he was a very spiritual person who had done a good job of bringing together his work and his faith. It certainly seemed to be true. He exuded peace, and what he had to say reflected a picture of someone who had put all the pieces together, starting at the core and working outward.

But I found that *he* saw the picture quite differently. For him, it was the frenzy of his work that forced him to become a more spiritual person and to get the rest of his life together. His work had been driving his life, taking more and more time, pushing aside family and friends. In response, he looked to the neglected spiritual side of his life and built a new way of working. He started doing spiritual exercises, at the beginning and at the end of his day, to help him keep a clear sense of the big picture. These steps had changed the way he worked at its most fundamental level. Despite being interviewed by a total stranger while handling calls in which thousands of dollars were at stake, he remained very calm. His maturity, grace, and presence beamed out in the midst of the chaos.

When I think about the worker who truly embodies the perspective of compassionate engagement, this man keeps coming to my mind. He works daily in the midst of the chaos of our world. He deals every moment with work conditions that are rapidly changing, customer focused, information-based, and owner-worker driven. His workplace is stressful to say the least. Yet he has found his way to peace within it, a peace driven by vision and character.

The term that best describes this man's attitude is *critical openness,* paradoxical as that may sound. He is carefully *critical*, in the sense that he analyzes his approach to work and to the world. *And* he has fostered an *openness* to the transcendent in the midst of his work. I call this is a paradox because we normally think of people as being *either* critical or open. That is, when I think about people who are consistently and carefully analytical in their approach to life, many of them are not prepared to welcome transcendent otherness through prayer or other actions of the open heart. Conversely, when I think of those who foster openness of heart, many of these people (though not all, of course) are anything but critically analytical of the world around them. But this man has brought together both a careful criticism of the world around him and an openness to the on going experience of transcendence.

This paradox bothers me. At one time, I was convinced that our task as soul-oriented workers was simply to become more compassionate and more open to transcendence. However, as I have worked with my model over the years, I have come to see that it requires far more. Especially as we struggle with the negatives of our work (as we shall see in the next chapter), we must become more critically analytical and more consciously alert to what is happening in and around us. In other words, I now believe we must grow in *two* directions – in our openness to the transcendent and in our ability to think critically – that sometimes seem incompatible and contradictory.

But in this man I begin to see how they come together. We can, as his life demonstrates, both critically evaluate ourselves and our world, and, at the same time, begin to experience the One who lives at the heart of all things. In fact, we *must* do both.

Fortunately, we can train ourselves in both critical thinking and openness. We can learn them, and then apply them to our lives.

Fortunately, we can train ourselves in both critical thinking and openness. We can learn them, and then apply them to our lives.

Critical Thinking

Critical thinking is one of the most important skills we can learn in order to become more sacred people. For a variety of reasons, however, critical thinking has gained a bad reputation in many circles. Too many people think of it as negative, excessively analytical, or even condemning. But critical thinking is not negative, and can even be a liberating and positive source of energy and good feeling. Yes, it can be misused, but so can any tool. The key is proper application, and when we learn proper application, we can open our lives in revolutionary ways to the presence of the sacred.

Critical thinking consists of two things: paying attention to assumptions, and being clear about *how* we think. Assumptions are those unquestioned premises, hopes, fears, and beliefs that underlie every aspect of the way we approach the world. Clarity about thinking means paying attention to the way we organize our thoughts and come to conclusions about the world. Together, they allow us to see how we actually work and relate to the world around us.

In other words, critical thinking provides the foundation from which we can carry out an effective campaign of personal change. It gives us the ability to overcome obstacles and transform institutions.

Assumptions

Underlying all of our thinking and perceptions are sets of assumptions, many of which are tied to our frames of reference. These assumptions can be as mundane as believing that the traffic rules will be the same today as they were yesterday, and as awesome as believing that the universe is built around the principle of love. If our assumptions are accurate, they will allow us to interact effectively with those around us. If our assumptions are false, they will cause us problems.

Although they are fewer in number today than they used to be, some people believe that it is possible to move beyond the level of assumption to observable, "objective" fact. Yet almost always, when these "objective" facts are analyzed, we discover that they are a combination of theory, frame of reference, and more or less substantial experience, organized through language. In other words, all "objective" facts come from people who have foundational assumptions, limited language, and profoundly selected experience. Therefore, their "objectivity" is really a better or worse representation of our common experience rooted in untested assumptions. Careful analysis tells us that, at a certain level, *all* we have are assumptions.

Because our assumptions play such a significant role in shaping relationships and our experience of the world, detecting and analyzing them is a vitally important critical skill. Those who can perceive the assumptions at work in any given situation can analyze them for accuracy, evidence, and truth. Once analyzed, we will know better where our perspective is strong and where it is weak, and, perhaps, when it should be changed.

The way to begin detecting assumptions is to start asking questions. What do these terms mean? What does each word in a statement refer to? How is it being used? What emotions are being brought into our conversation through our choice of words (and there are always emotions attached to words)?

The real purpose of examining our assumptions is so that we can suggest or discover alternatives.

When I define work as beginning with imagination, for example, what do I mean by "beginning" and "imagination"? What if I said instead that work is "rooted in our fantasies"? While the statement might be true, it has a very different sense of emotion to it and becomes, I suspect, less plausible. Therefore, in my choice of terms, I am making some assumptions about the best way to write about the processes of the brain, which I believe underlie all human endeavor. But it doesn't end there. My words also assume that all work has its source in each working person and therefore that everyone has an imagination. Yet there are those who would question both the individualism and the understanding of human brain being assumed. They might prefer to assume that work always represents the action of a group and that only some humans have imaginations.

The real purpose of examining our assumptions is so that we can suggest or discover alternatives. For example, at one point, the car broker analyzed his commute and realized that his assumption that it could be nothing more than a mundane process of getting to and from work might not be true. So he explored alternatives to that assumption and discovered that, if properly approached, it could be a time for prayer. He then tested this alternative assumption and found it to be true.

This book itself represents an example of the process of analyzing and changing assumptions. One of the foundational assumptions of our industrial world has been that work belongs to some "secular" aspect of our existence, and that the inner person is where the "sacred" resides. Instead, I asked myself, "What if the inner and outer are one, and even the most ordinary and mundane work has a sacred aspect?" Based on that changed assumption, I began to see new relationships between parts of my life that were previously disconnected, and subsequently developed new strategies for working.

Once we understand our assumptions, we are freed to choose new paths that reflect assumptions we believe to be "truer."

Thinking Clearly

The other side of critical thinking involves paying attention to the "how" of our thinking. For example, it does not take much reflection to recognize that all of our thinking has an emotional aspect to it. We feel better and worse, depending on how we think about things. (Do we see events as *opportunities* or as *problems*?)

Around every word and concept, we hold a halo of emotion. These emotions change the way we respond to the world around us. One word sends us into a frenzy, another calms us down. We learn these associations between words and emotions on the basis of past experience and the example of others. Once those associations have been established, it is easy for us to fall victim to their influence; they can move us without our conscious agreement. On the other hand, if we attend to the emotions that go with the words, we gain insight into ourselves and into how we understand the world to truly be. We become more able to see *past* the words and into the heart of things. This does not mean that the emotion goes away; it does not. But it *does* mean that we can begin to understand and choose our responses; we can take greater control of ourselves and therefore of our environment. We can also communicate more effectively with others.

In the same way that the words and concepts we use always have an emotional aspect, so too, our "thought world" is loaded with logical fallacies. These are errors in thinking – ways of thinking that are not rooted in verifiable relationships between concepts.

It is easy for us to become trapped in negative or useless thinking on the basis of fallacies. Fallacies are also a way others attempt to control our behavior. Some of the most common fallacies are appeals to emotion (when we should be outlining evidence), *post hoc* analysis (drawing conclusions after the fact that are based on spurious links), and black-and-white thinking (something is either one *or* the other, without the possibility of alternatives or paradox). Clarity of thinking requires that we become alert to the fallacies in our thoughts and in the thoughts of others, and do our best to root them out. Usually, fallacies represent a form of dishonesty and the world suffers as a result.

Clear thinking is essential if we are to understand who we are and what we are capable of doing.

Finally, we need to be aware that there are many "styles" or "forms" of thinking, each with its own strengths and weaknesses. There is logical thinking, with its deductive and inductive processes. But there are other forms of thinking, with rules for appropriate application and use. One such form is narrative thinking: thinking from initial conditions, to action and climax, and then to end conditions. Related to narrative thinking is chronological thinking: the thinking we do whenever we focus on time itself and the mechanical division of existence into seconds, hours, days, years, and millennia. Intuition is a form of reasoning that extrapolates from small data sets to long-term conclusions. All these forms of thinking happen all the time. Each one can be improved through attention to its strengths and by understanding its correct application.

Clear thinking is essential if we are to understand who we are and what we are capable of doing. It's like personal cleanliness, or practiced driving; we can do more, cause less damage in the doing, and maintain a better quality of life if we can think clearly. Attending to the emotions in *our* words and the words of *others* brings us self-control and reduces the damage we accidentally do. Attending to fallacies helps to keep us from being mislead and makes us clearer in our communications with others. Using the correct form of reasoning makes us more able to conceptually organize what is happening around us and more effective in responding to it.

It is difficult, in such a short space, to appropriately emphasize how powerful it is to be able to think critically. All the ability we may possess to know and experience the presence of the Ultimate, let alone our goals and commitments, cannot overcome the results of our poor thinking. Without critical thinking, we are like chittering monkeys leaping about. We may have captivating things to say and do, but we run the risk of being misled by every glittering distraction around us, and our thoughts will be poorly organized, unpersuasive, and implicitly dishonest. On the other hand, once we begin to perceive our assumptions and attend to our thinking, we are able to be more honest with ourselves and with others about what we are experiencing, perceiving, and deciding. I am convinced that critical thinking is an essential part of interpersonal accountability, and a vital tool on the road to soul work.

DISCIPLINES FOR OPENNESS

Openness is much more complex than critical thinking. We live at many levels and engage the world around us at many levels. This means that if we are to foster openness, we must learn abilities at all of the levels we engage in the workplace. We might call some of these abilities "spiritual." Some relate to our need to find and foster community. Others foster our physical well-being. Once we have gained these abilities, we become open to the breath of life that flows within and around us.

Spiritual Disciplines

As I talk to those who move effectively through their workplace chaos, I find they have one thing in common. They all pray – pray, or meditate, or do centering exercises. Most start their working day with prayer. Some do centering exercises on the way *to* work, or *at* work, or on the way home *from* work. The car broker meditates as he drives to work. An executive I know starts her day with a litany. A consultant takes little breaks, just a few seconds long, throughout his day, to center himself. Each of these exercises has the same effect: it brings the "doer" back to his or her center, back to the big picture, back to the why and how of their work.

It is no easy thing to pray, particularly when we think of prayer as formal, memorized words, or as requiring careful concentration. My mentor taught me to "hold" thoughts and images briefly in mind, bringing their being into my being for just a few seconds.

Many people associate prayer with childhood table graces, or long periods of silent meditation. They fail to see that spiritual centering can take place in the middle of the workday. But opening ourselves to the possibility of prayer at any moment can be done, and when it *is* done, it changes us profoundly. By learning new models of prayer that fit the way we live our lives, we can gain the grounding we need when we need it.

Flash Prayers

A mentor once taught me a technique, which he referred to as "flash prayers." We had been discussing how to pray in the midst of day-to-day activity. It is no easy thing to pray, particularly when we think of prayer as formal, memorized words, or as requiring careful concentration. My mentor taught me to "hold" thoughts and images briefly in mind, bringing *their* being into *my* being for just a few seconds. In this way, we can learn to feel and act with respect to the sacred in that moment.

Now, when I am going into a meeting, I pause just for a moment and take a deep breath. While slowly exhaling, I turn my attention inward and focus on my muscles, imagining what it is like for my heart to be beating at that moment. Then I take a second breath, and on the exhale I imagine the faces of those I am meeting with, or one of the people I am meeting with, and try to feel and honor their sacredness. All it takes is two or three breaths, and my relationship to those I am meeting with has changed.

Of course, the feeling this engenders is fleeting. We cannot live in this state very long. We are always caught up in what is happening around us and we lose that attention almost immediately. But then, in the midst of the meeting, I *remember* that exercise and it reminds me to honor my spirit, the spirit of those in the room, and the sacred presence that flows in and through each one of us.

I notice that these flash prayers often have the very practical effect of keeping me calmer. As well, they help me to see things from the point of view of others in the room, a necessary part of creating constructive relationships. Most importantly, sometimes they help me to see the way we need to work together to find the common good.

I can also use flash prayers to remind myself of the community outside of the workplace. These people, too, can be brought to mind and honored in those fleeting seconds I can find here and there during the workday. Wherever I am, in tiny moments, the sacred can emerge, if only I "flash" myself open to it.

Repetitive Prayers

Repetitive prayers are another technique some use to find the sacred in the midst of the day to day. Thinking up a prayer, or finding the right method of meditation for any given moment can be hard, and to make prayer easier many people repeat a brief phrase. It may be something they have written. It may be taken from a powerful poem or a sacred scripture or come from one of the many religious traditions. The point is to find a line, a few words, that say something important about our relationship to the essence of the universe.

As the person praying slowly learns to hear, in the repeated words, the essence of the universe, and begins to change in response, the words come alive.

In the Orthodox tradition of Christianity, the Jesus prayer uses repetition to do just that. The one praying repeats over and over the line, "God have mercy on me, a sinner." In this prayer, the Orthodox worshipper is called to affirm a basic understanding of his or her relationship to the universe, and opens him or herself to that source of spiritual energy.

By repeating this line in the midst of the day, we recall the big picture and are brought back to a grounding point. As repetition wears it into our lives, it becomes a point of reassurance, and a window into the universe as it "really" is.

There are many other such prayers; most non-Western traditions have them. Repetition has long been known as a way of moving out of the ordinary and into the spiritual, and even in the workplace this exercise can have an effect. Repetition seeks to make us aware of the essence of the sacred. It brings us out of ourselves and the transience around us, and back into the presence of our unchanging core.

The one drawback of these prayers is that they can take years to become fully effective. As the person praying slowly learns to hear, in the repeated words, the essence of the universe, and begins to change in response, the words come alive. After many years of practice, repetitive prayer can have an almost instantaneous calming and centering effect.

Devotional Practices

Devotions are structured prayers or periods of meditation, which are often anchored around repetitive features in the day. One executive I know has a routine she follows every day at work. She follows a pattern of readings and prayer based on the Bible, including prayers used by the church throughout history. Every weekday morning, she reads the scripture text selected for that day and then follows with a prayer selected for the time of day and season of the year. The details change, but the daily routine is the same.

Devotional practices are much more complex than repetitive prayers, but they still function to ground the person using them. They require access to spiritual resources, often take years to develop, as one piece gets added to another to form an empowering whole.

Symbols

Visual images can be powerful cues as well. Most of us have some personal memento in our workplace, very often a picture of our family or life partner. Similarly, we can use symbols to remind us of what is essential to our lives. Images of saints, nature, or special symbols discreetly placed in our workplace can remind us who we really are and what we are really trying to accomplish in a larger sense. Though candles, incense, and various aromatics are inappropriate to most workplace settings, they can be helpful, too. The key in each case is to find something that throws us out of our everyday consciousness and that helps us remember what is important.

Centering Exercises

Centering exercises can be an ongoing part of work life, or something used in times of stress. There are any number of these exercises, but what they all have in common is "attending." Attending to the rhythm of our breathing – paying attention to *how* we inhale and exhale, and the *rate* at which we do it – is particularly common. As you do this, the tension dissolves in the rest of your body, with the effect that you are more relaxed and alert, and more sensitive to the issues confronting you.

Often, breathing or attending exercises are combined with visualization exercises. Visualization helps us fix certain thoughts or images in mind to assist in internal clarification. One visualization technique I use under times of extreme stress is to imagine behaving calmly and competently in the midst of my work. From that image, I can often gain a better sense of perspective, while at the same time the breathing exercise calms me inwardly. I may not become the person I wish I was, but for the moment I can take a few steps in that direction.

WORKPLACE COMMUNITY

Community is a difficult word to use these days. Often our lives seem so transient that real connection and intimacy is difficult to find. Talking about workplace community is even more difficult. Our workplaces focus on tasks, rather than on tasks *and* relationships. How, then, do we open our workplaces to the type of community that will help us live well? For that is what it is about: finding openness to our humanity, our common hopes, fears, and needs, in the context of our work.

For some, this question is not important. Some of us have such a strong family, or so many good friends, that the need to find community in the workplace does not seem urgent. But for many of us, work is one of the few places of continuity in our lives. In the midst of variety and transience, those we work with become the important constants. Particularly when our families and most important relationships are shattered by crisis, the workplace is one place we turn to for community.

As we strive to become more whole as people in our work, how can we build the type of community that heals and helps? Asking this question is key to finding a community of fellow-travelers in our workplace, a group of people moving with us on the journey of our lives. Learning how to do it is critical.

The first step is to learn to work together. This may seem obvious. For many of us, it is already so normal that we do not even think about it. We go about being supportive and friendly to those we work with, assisting others, and going out of our way to make the workplace a comfortable environment. However, not all workplaces function this way. But by working together we can make even the most difficult workplaces more humane.

Be Polite and Friendly

Working together to create community starts with our attitude to one another. Polite friendliness is a good starting place; it goes a long way in opening a workplace to community. A balance of politeness and friendliness can create a space in which trust will grow. Having this attitude toward everyone, regardless of whether or not they deserve it, has a tremendous impact on our relationships. It opens us up to trusting and caring for each other. It makes difficult circumstances easier. It creates an environment open to communication.

Together, politeness and friendliness allow distance and approach, and a comfortable environment for others to choose a response. While they may not bring us the intimacy we may be looking for, they go a long way toward creating a healthy and healing workplace.

Communicate Clearly

Clarity in our communication is a second strategy we can use to build workplace community. "Let our yes mean yes, and our no mean no," is an admonition we have all heard before. Yet we all too easily forget how important it is. Being clear about what we can or cannot do, will or will not do, is essential for building trust and cooperation. Often our tendency is to inflate some of our capabilities, and to underrate others, particularly when doing so will provide us with an advantage. We may try to meet other people's expectations even when those expectations are out of line with reality. But to build trust and community, we must be clear about our intentions and abilities. Only when other people find a coherence between our words

The first step is to learn to work together. This may seem obvious. For many of us, it is already so normal that we do not even think about it.

and our actions will they trust our words. Naturally, we tend to respect and want to be around those who are open about their strengths and weaknesses, and give realistic appraisals of their work. Deadlines agreed to and met can build powerful bonds between people. Quality levels agreed to and achieved create a solid working foundation. They also build trust. If what you say is accurate in one area, then I am likely to believe what you have to say in another area.

We can never overestimate the impact of clarity of communication on a workplace. Once someone takes the risk of being clear about their intentions, once someone demonstrates coherence between their words and their deeds, relationships change. Immediately, a new standard of behavior emerges, one which encourages everyone into being more coherent, more honest, and more open. For most people, a positive pattern of communication grows to the point where it becomes hard to resist.

I have found that this level of communication is also an excellent marketing tool. My first strategy with a potential customer is to be completely clear about what I can do, how I will do it, and when it can be done. I also inform the customer about what I will *not* do, and why. I do this using simple, straightforward language. Most of the time, I find that the potential customer opens up to me and becomes more honest about what they are looking for, saving both of us time and money. Sometimes I can assist the customer in deciding what they want, giving me a huge competitive advantage. Even when I do not get the contract, I have left the door open to effective future conversations.

Of course, there are two sides to this. It does not work if your attempt at honesty and clarity is met with resistance. One work group I know about tried to tell their vice-president that the new database system they were working on would not be ready by its target date. But rather than working with the work group to understand, the vice-president told the group that the program *would* be ready by the target, and that he would inform the president of that fact immediately. The group, despite best efforts, was nowhere close to completion when the program was announced. So the work group ran out a small portion of their new system calling it "Phase 1," even though it had yet to be debugged and could not function without the rest of the system. Other than the vice-president, no one was satisfied. Morale was shot, tempers frayed all around, and operators were given an unusable system.

Listen

This points to a third strategy for creating workplace community: listening. Healing and health can only occur through listening. Perhaps "attending" might be a better word, because listening is usually about words, and the behavior I am describing has as much to do with observing and responding, as it does with hearing words. Building healthy community involves listening to the life of the workplace, listening to what is going on behind the words of each person. When I speak, I am communicating at least two different kinds of messages. One message is the content of what I am saying and is found in the words. The second message has to do with what it means to me and is found in my tone of voice and the body language. Of the two messages, the second is most important to community. In our tone of voice, the way we stand or hold our hands, our level of muscle tension, we indicate our inner state, our relationship to the others in the conversation, the level of urgency we feel, and a thousand other things. While a person's words may be about work issues, the non-verbal signals may indicate hope for the future, disdain for a colleague, urgency toward a task, worry about a child, or pleasure in the view outside the window. Good community happens when we attend to the full range of communication and learn to discern and respond to its non-verbal aspects. Attending to non-verbal cues can prompt us to ask, "Is there something else?" when we detect an underlying concern.

Attending-type listening does not stop with individuals. It is also something we need to learn to do with groups. Suppose that one work group you meet with bubbles with enthusiasm all the time, while another group may be much quieter. It may be that there are two different work styles in action. Or perhaps there are problems in one of the work groups. By attending to the differences, we can pick up on details, ask questions, and learn what is really going on.

One acquaintance told me that when he took over his department he immediately noticed some sort of problem in the way the men and women were responding to each other. He could feel it, but he could not name the source of it. He could not understand what was happening until he made a trip to the women's washroom. Sexist graffiti covered the walls; some of it had been there for years. Having made that discovery, he could begin to address the issues it represented and build a better working environment.

Work groups develop their own language and patterns of communication. Habits become ingrained and new workers soon learn the non-verbal rules of the group. These patterns can be as obvious as two groups of people refusing to talk to each other, or as subtle as using a particular unspoken way to reward creativity. Good listening means attending to all forms of communication.

Setting Work-Group Vision

One highly powerful way of creating workplace community is to foster group vision. All of us need a sense of what our work is pushing toward. Is it to have the best customer service in the mall? Or is it about "redefining compassion," as one social service agency proclaims? We need a sense of the big picture in order to feel good about what we do. Sometimes corporations circulate their "big picture" in a mission statement, which everyone in the organization feels part of. When this is not the case, it falls on us as workers to proclaim such a vision. As those who care about healing and health, we need to proclaim a vision for our work. It may encompass the whole company, or just relate to our smaller area of responsibility.

Merely proclaiming such a vision is not enough. It must be demonstrated. This means telling stories about how particular work actions brought the vision to life and saying, "Well done," when someone's actions reflect the vision.

Accountability Groups

But what if the workplace itself is not conducive to community? Perhaps employees work off-site, or on different shifts. The car broker, who spends almost all of his time on the phone, uses an accountability group to build community. The accountability group is a group of people who voluntarily get together, often early in the morning, to talk, share, and find support.

In the accountability group, members pledge to be honest. They agree to be open about what they are feeling, thinking, and doing. In turn, the group agrees to support the individual, to confront him or her gently when the group sees a need for confrontation, and to assist each other in personal and professional growth. Larger employers sometimes find these groups springing up among co-workers. The group the car broker is part of consists of people he has known for many years, plus a few others that the various members have more recently met. These folk get together every week or so over breakfast, to talk, share, and journey together.

Unless we allow them to, very few people outside of our families know much about us. This fact of urban life drives accountability groups. We rarely have the opportunity to react to the heart issues of a wide range of people, and therefore have little opportunity to learn from them. Not making ourselves vulnerable and allow-ing people to see and react to us as we really are may make life easier in many respects, but it deprives us of many opportunities for growth as persons. Accountability or support groups help us move away from the surface of our lives to see their deeper struc-tures. Because they are not as close to us as family, accountability groups can sometimes see our lives more clearly and suggest how we might become more effective.

Diet & Exercise

One of the separations we tend to make in our lives is between diet and work. We tend to think of diet in terms of health, forget-ting that health has a great deal to do with our ability to function well at work. When I interviewed the car broker, I noticed that he didn't drink coffee or a soft drink, but rather mineral water. He was attending to his well-being through what he took into himself.

Many people find that as they begin to take care of themselves, certain parts of their diet naturally change. Coffee and doughnuts, dietary staples in many workplaces, are not the types of food that generate peace in the workplace. Their high chemical (coffee is a soup of complex and powerful chemicals, of which caffeine is only the most well-known), fat, and sugar content changes brain and body chemistry. Attending to the spirit is much more difficult when we stuff the body with the wrong foods.

What we put into our bodies has a profound effect on what we produce. High fiber foods, a vegetarian or at least low-meat diet, and lots of water improve our ability to think, pray, and act. Eating more fruits and vegetables can make us more effective spiritually (and in every other way). I find yogurt to be extremely helpful for re-establishing body equilibrium. Cut back or eliminate high-fat foods, meats (especially red meat), coffee, and alcohol. Abstaining can mean social isolation in some workplaces and it may not fit well with critical parts of work life (meals with customers, for example). In these cases, giving care and attention to other parts of our diet during other times of day may be adequate.

Exercise is also crucial to our physical and spiritual well-being. Our bodies need to be in reasonably good physical shape if we are to think, pray, or act well.

Exercise is also crucial to our physical and spiritual well-being. Our bodies need to be in reasonably good physical shape if we are to think, pray, or act well. Getting 20 minutes of physical exercise every couple of days is a good idea for everyone and going for a walk over lunch is a good way to begin. For years, I walked to and from work, a brisk 20-minute walk each way. I could not do it every day due to the weather, but most days it was not a problem. The level of well-being those walks engendered in me cannot be overestimated. I felt better, thought better, and did better work. We need to keep ourselves moving in order to function well at every level of our being.

Rest and Sleep

Much like diet, rest is an often neglected part of work life. The ancients, it appears, knew a lot about the importance of rest – things we have largely forgotten. I was amazed to find in my reading of the Bible, for example, that the subject of work is usually found in the context of rest. In the world of the ancient Israelites, rest from work was a sign of God's blessing. In the story of the creation of the world, which is told in the biblical book of Genesis, God creates the world in six days. At the end of each day, God looks at what has been created and declares it "good." At the end of the sixth day, God looks at *all* the work of the previous six days and declares it "very good." Then, on the seventh day, God rests (Genesis 1:1–23).

The ability to rest was a sign that the world reflected God's ideal. Not only that, rest becomes *part* of that ideal. God blesses the seventh day, the Sabbath, and declares it holy. This idea becomes so important that a later tradition even states that if only all Jews would keep the Sabbath one time, then the kingdom of God would come.

Rest speaks of the holy. We need it, if we are to become fully spiritual and whole beings.

In our machine modeled culture, this ancient wisdom has often been obscured. We describe rest the way we describe the breakdown of a machine – in terms of "downtime." We tend to see the need for rest as a sign of weakness. Our attitudes to sleep are not much different. We praise people who get by on less than eight hours of sleep, as if they were somehow more virtuous. I know of one industry consultant who delights in describing sleep – only half jokingly – as a "bourgeois affectation" and who takes great pride in the fact that he only needs four hours of sleep a night. Anyone who regularly gets eight hours of sleep may even be called "lazy." Yet it is clear that regular and adequate sleep has an immediate impact on our ability to work. One study indicates that the effects of sleep deprivation are cumulative and that even tiny amounts of sleep deprivation – as little as one hour per night – immediately reduce intelligence as measured by IQ, and that high levels of sleep deprivation lead to sloppiness, impaired judgment, accident, and injury.

We need regular sleep – usually eight hours of sleep for full functioning. This often means going to bed earlier and cutting out some non-work activity. For those who take work home with them, it may mean letting some things go undone. While this may be hard to do at first, well-rested people can work much more effectively and efficiently, and in most cases the decrease in hours worked is more than made up for.

If you cannot get eight hours of sleep at night, try napping. Even short naps have a powerful rejuvenating effect.

Rest also involves taking breaks from our work. Our bodies and minds respond better to working for shorter periods of time on a variety of tasks, than for longer periods of time on a single task. We need to move from chore to chore, and stretch and rest in between. These breaks restore our judgment, assist our insight, and bring back our ability to concentrate. Taking a break from our work allows our mental energies to regroup and when we come back we often find that a difficult problem has solved itself.

So far, I have really only described the physiological need for and benefits of rest. But rest and sleep are important parts of spirituality as well. In my own life, rest played a role in shaping who I am. Even though I have sometimes been called a workaholic, rest is fundamentally important to my working spirituality. No matter how hard I work, I know that without the appropriate sleep I will begin to disconnect means from ends, and the truly meaningful from the irrelevant. Without enough sleep, I lose the ability to attend to myself and others compassionately.

As well, sleep brings dreams, and dreams are also important to our well-being. They tell us things about ourselves and our relationships that are otherwise sometimes hard to see. Sometimes they confirm things we already suspected. During one stressful period in my life, I dreamed a particular pattern of dream over and over. Eventually, I began to see that the structure of the dream reflected my work. Even though the images were fantastic (flight engineer on a crash landing space shuttle), the basic pattern of the dream revealed my work situation. Indeed, at that time I was not in control of my work, but was trying hard to keep a highly destructive organization operational.

Truthfully, I do not always attend to my dreams. They often have to break through with a repeated pattern or a particularly vivid image before I begin to puzzle over them. But I cannot ignore that in my dreams essential parts of my work may come to my attention.

Daydreams are important, too. When we day-dream, we allow our minds to wander down paths that mean something to us, paths which may include our work. The content of our work daydreams may tell us something about our values; we may gain a clearer vision of ourselves, or find a source of inspiration. When we daydream, we open another channel through which the spirit can speak to us.

The ancient Jews recognized that not only people *need* rest, but the land *does, too.*

Rest helps us become more gentle with our tasks and with our colleagues. In our usual states of rush and exhaustion, patience and care can get pushed aside. But when we are well-rested, we tend to be more patient and willing to live with our work and our colleagues, and we have a greater capacity to attend to the details of our work. Rest allows us to *create* harmony in the workplace to bring our work to proper completion.

There is yet another side to work, which benefits from rest. The ancient Jews recognized that not only *people* need rest, but the *land* does, too. And so Sabbatical laws stipulated that every seven years the land should lie fallow for a year. They saw the world around them as having its own life, with its own rhythms and needs. Today, in some places on the prairies, where fields have been planted and harvested year after year with little break, the soil has become damaged and erosion has become a major prob-lem. Likewise, many of our forests are in need of rest from heavy logging, and some of our fish stocks from overfishing. Today, the world around us needs a Sabbatical rest as much as it ever has.

Yet this is not just true of ecological systems, which need the opportunity to recover equilibrium. Even in a technological and urban environment, our work needs to be attended to within its own pattern of activity and rest. Sometimes our work needs a rest from us as much as we need a rest from it. This is particularly true for managers and for activities such as planning and evaluation, and for tasks related to human development and community activity. Sometimes, our work creates a dynamic that twists relationships out of shape and we need to back off so that these relationships can regain equilibrium. Sometimes, people perform better when managers oversee and meddle less.

Allowing ourselves to rest from our work and our work to rest from us is essential. At the very least, we come back to our work with new eyes. But sometimes, in our absence, the work reveals itself and we come back to find something other than what we left.

We lose much when we ignore rest. We fill our working days with frenetic activity and long lists of mundane tasks and then wonder why we are tired and the important things never seem to get done. When we rest, the truth can emerge.

Hope

What I have tried to outline here are a series of exercises, skills, tools, and techniques that will provide us with what I like to think of as "correct posture." Equipped with this posture, we have the ability to much more effectively engage the world around us and to have our work reflect our deepest commitments. We begin to see and are able to respond to aspects of existence within us that are necessary for true participation in our world.

I like to think of these abilities as the posture of *hope*. By this I mean that they are the signs of a personal stance (like an ergonomically correct workstation) that enables us to work more effectively and healthily for the long-term. Once we have them, we know we can look into the future with commitment and clarity. We know that while we may not master our world, we are at least more capable of engaging it effectively, deeply, and honestly. And therefore we have hope.

Hope, I believe, is one of the divine attributes. The forces that underlie all existence are rooted in and flow out of hope: the future can be better than the present. There is real potential for a better future rooted in the fabric of the cosmos. When we live "hope-fully", we align ourselves with the deepest fabric of existence. In hope, we enter our souls. In hope, we are prepared to fabricate the world as it should be.

We begin to see and are able to respond to aspects of existence within us that are necessary for true participation in our world.

8

Struggle

Confronting the Darkness

A number of years ago I met the senior manager of a large company. He had started working for this company right after high school and had earned one degree and almost completed a second in his spare time. He was well-respected, an able trouble-shooter, and was regularly called in to help divisions experiencing problems. Staff usually spoke very highly of him.

When I met him, I was stunned by the contrast between the man I had heard about and the one I saw. While he was superficially charming to talk to and seemed to demonstrate competence, it seemed as if a choking cloud of depressing blackness hovered around him. Our initial conversation was twisted and confusing. He appeared at least ten years older than he was. He was also in extremely poor health and I feared that at any moment he might collapse. It did not help that

When our work becomes destructive of ourselves, our colleagues, or our environment, we need to address the factors that make it so.

he was chain smoking and drinking his way into a stupor at the time.

I got the impression that this man was a destroyer, not a creator. The hackles on my neck tingled the whole time I was with him and I felt "slimy" after he left. Despite his good reputation, he struck me as the most "evil" person I had ever met.

I met him again ten years later and I was amazed at the change. The black cloud was gone. While his health was still poor, he seemed in much better shape than I remembered. He was certainly clearer and more positive. While I would not call our conversation enjoyable, it did not leave me with bad feelings.

I learned, for example, that he had taken early retirement after 40 years of what he regarded as hell. He had hated his job – hated what he had to do, and hated the way the company worked. The black cloud was not him, but his job.

I also learned why he had been so effective in his job, and why I had been so shocked by the contrast between his reputation and the man I met. He had internalized all the things he had hated in order to protect others. He had worked hard to ensure that others did not experience the company the way he did and he was trusted for it. That internalization was what made him the man I thought of as "evil." Without the job, the evil dropped away.

The Workplace Is Never Neutral

Our work is never neutral. It either helps us to become better people, and the world to become a better place, or it makes us and the world worse. Regardless of the intentions we bring to it or the position we have, our work shapes us and the world around us in very powerful ways.

When our work becomes destructive of ourselves, our colleagues, or our environment, we need to address the factors that make it so. The senior manager referred to above addressed the negative factors in the workplace, but in a way that was as destructive as the factors themselves. He abused his health, punished his family, and wasted a huge portion of his life in a bottle, in an attempt to deal with the demands of his work. When he finally made the *important* change – that of leaving the job – his whole being changed for the better. I can only wonder what would have happened had he left the job years earlier. What could he have achieved in a more positive environment? His story is tragic because he could have chosen another path.

NAMING THE DARKNESS

The first step in addressing the destructive side – or the dark side or shadow side – of our work is to name it. Naming reduces the power of the shadow side over us, and gives us the power to change it.

We must be very careful *how* we deal with what we find destructive in our environment. It is easy to see evil where it does not exist, and to miss it where it does. We need to understand ethics and power, organizational dynamics, and our personal "shadow." We need to be sensitive to how those forces that ground existence use pain and suffering to open new possibilities for goodness and growth. We need to be sensitive to how striving for perfection can cause unnecessary pain and suffering for ourselves and for those around us. The struggle we commit ourselves to in order to compassionately engage our world is very complex and it is to understanding it that we turn now.

The first step in addressing the destructive side – or the dark side or shadow side – of our work is to name it. Naming reduces the power of the shadow side over us, and gives us the power to change it. Naming enables us to identify the problem so we might see what type of change is appropriate. Naming connects us to what others have experienced and done, and shows us the place of our problem in the context of the human community. It keeps us from running from the problem, or from participating in activities that make the problem worse. But naming a problem is really only half the solution.

The challenge is to name things *accurately*. Improper naming leads to misdirected actions and to "solutions" that are not solutions at all. One highway authority decided to crack down on speeders, having decided that there were far too many people driving above the posted limit on a particular section of highway. This raised quite an outcry. To the surprise of many, the highway authority then reviewed the situation and decided that, in this case, the problem was not too many people speeding, but a speed limit that was too low. They had originally misnamed the problem and, under review, determined that people could drive considerably faster without risk on the identified section of highway. The speed limit was raised, with few negative consequences.

Misnaming of problems happens all too often in the workplace, particularly when it comes to personnel issues.

Misnaming of problems happens all too often in the workplace, particularly when it comes to personnel issues. A former employee of mine told me, after we had worked together for some time, that she had been fired from her previous job. Management had named her as the problem in the office. Her "crime" had been a bad attitude and they had decided that the solution was to remove her. This surprised me, since I knew her as a positive, cheerful, and diligent staff member. While I cannot be sure, since I was not involved in the situation, I suspect that management had misnamed the problem and that they had, in the process, let go of one of their best staff. (She was, as I say, one of the pillars of our department.)

Large bureaucracies are especially noted for this sort of thing. An engineer in a large company discovered one day that a number of major customers were routinely overpaying their energy bills due to a problem in the type of meter the company was using. Under a specific set of circumstances, the meter consistently read the usage at a higher-than-actual rate. It took him two years to have the problem recognized by senior management, and he was nearly fired in the process. His division manager, refusing to accept that the meter was the problem, was inclined to believe that the *engineer* was the problem. Word eventually got out, however, and the meters were replaced. (Management also balked at reimbursing its customers for the overpayment.)

Some problems, of course, are genuinely confusing. We can face situations where there are so many issues involved that accurate naming becomes next to impossible. Once, I bravely attacked a complex problem in church life only to decide a year later that it was virtually "unsolvable." There were so many factors in play – matters of geography, finances, ethnicity, building structure, and tradition – that I was never sure I had really named the problem.

It is imperative, when we look at the destructive aspects of our work, that we do our best to name the root problems.

It is imperative, when we look at the destructive aspects of our work, that we do our best to name the root problems. This is *really* what accurate naming is all about.

Inertia and Resistance

One problem we might face and name is inertia. No matter who we are, or how powerful, we are enmeshed in complex systems. These systems –work, friends, family – have their own understandings of who we are in relation to them, and of right and wrong. As we grow and change, these systems will react. Sometimes they will push back – hard. This is resistance: "You *can't* do it that way!" Other times, they won't do anything in response to the changing situation. "This is the way we have always worked together." In other words, their "response" will be inertia.

Take this problem seriously, but not too seriously. This is generally not an evil set on interfering with our pursuit of the good. Often, resistance and inertia emerge out of the good will of those around us, but a good will that is not prepared to go as far as we are. Resistance and inertia can even be a good thing that helps keep excessive enthusiasm in check. Still, in their extreme forms, resistance and inertia can be much more negative.

Whether we meet them in their milder or extreme forms, resistance and inertia will be something we face, no matter how good the things may be that flow out of our compassionate engagement. The only response we can make is gentle persistence. Once we understand where our souls are taking us in our work, it is more often a matter of taking constant slow steps, as if into a strong wind, than it is of making rapid, unimpeded progress. Yes, sometimes we see great vistas, and massive changes follow upon our visions. But gentle steps are what eradicate resistance and change inertia.

Gentle steps are what eradicate resistance and change inertia.

Character Problems (lying, cheating, stealing)

Another problem we all face at work is dealing with those who do not treat us properly or act appropriately. No matter how isolated we may be in our job, most of us have had some experience with people who lie, cheat, steal, or who are otherwise abusive. These experiences are discouraging at best and personally devastating at worst. If it were easy to identify these folk beforehand, perhaps they would be easier to deal with. But they are *not* easy to identify. Anyone can become a "problem" person in this regard, ourselves included.

While most of us treat each other reasonably well, all of us, from time to time, break the most basic rules of human conduct. Most of us do it out of hurt, stress, exhaustion, or illness. Our marriage is in trouble so our tempers flare and we end up yelling at a store clerk. Or we conclude that the management at work has taken advantage of us and so we feel justified in walking off with a couple hundred dollars of equipment. At times, our judgment is impaired and we do things that we later genuinely regret. These lapses of judgment are experienced quite differently by those on the receiving end. To them, our actions come across as abuse, violence, and misuse.

Our best personal response can be to commit ourselves to integrity and honesty. While this may not stop us from breaking the rules from time to time, it will give us the strength to apologize and to correct our behavior. Otherwise, one lapse can lead to another, and slowly we – and those around us – lose our civility.

While most of us treat each other reasonably well, all of us, from time to time, break the most basic rules of human conduct. Most of us do it out of hurt, stress, exhaustion, or illness.

Unfortunately, the general public seems to have decided that there are some contexts in which misuse and abuse are *acceptable*. An ex-civil servant once confided to me his reasons for leaving government. He said, "You know how civil servants get a beaten-down look? It is because people beat on us. I don't know what it is, but people think that because we work for the government they can abuse us. Being out of the service is wonderful. People say 'Please' and 'Thank you,' and they mean it!"

Then there are those people who violate the rules of trust and honesty on a regular basis. A favorite scam in our community is to show up at a business with a load of new photocopier toner cartridges. The cartridges are delivered and the bill presented. Usually, the bill is paid long before anyone is aware that the cartridges were not ordered. Sometimes no one ever discovers the fraud, and the unordered and very high-priced toner just becomes part of the stock. Sometimes the fraud is only discovered after someone tries them in the machine and finds that the machine no longer works properly due to toner incompatibility – a problem which can be very expensive to repair.

These problems are not easily addressed. Both the systematically abused civil servant and the fraud artist are caught in self-perpetuating systems. The difference is that the civil servant's situation is external, while the thief's situation is internal. Neither can be dealt with without major effort and support from a community. In these cases it may be best simply to walk away as cleanly as possible.

Addictions/Emotional Issues

Still more difficult to deal with are destructive personal problems. There are drug addicts, alcoholics, sex addicts, and people with serious personality disorders in the workplace. Each may have a serious destructive impact on the work environment. Typically, these people are abusive and yet somehow draw people into their needs and problems. They generally, though not always, do poor work, have high rates of absenteeism, and can be extremely hard to deal with. Sometimes they are the boss. Sometimes they are a key customer. Sometimes they are a colleague. Whoever they may be, few of us manage to avoid them altogether.

What makes these people hard to deal with is the way they manipulate those around them. Many people with serious problems are able to do just well enough to hang on to their jobs. They draw people around them who will cover up for their mistakes, assist them to meet deadlines, and feed them the emotional support they want. When confronted, they usually try to create a highly charged emotional environment. They become swirling vortexes, casting wider and wider circles of negative energy. In many cases, the drain becomes so immense that their supporters start to break down, or become dependent (co-dependent) upon the addict themselves.

Of course, it is natural for us to want to help. Yet if we get caught up in caring for these deeply troubled people, we are headed for trouble ourselves. They will demand more and more of us, until we have nothing left to give. While most of us (hopefully) are mature enough to take responsibility for our own actions, many of these people are not. They will do anything, including destroying those who care for them, in order to avoid taking responsibility for their own behavior.

Dealing with this type of a situation as a colleague, or worse yet, as an employee, is extremely difficult. It is sometimes hard to avoid becoming a supporter of the manipulator, or becoming conflicted with either the person or members of their circle.

The best strategy is to maintain your focus. Be very clear about your work and what you are trying to achieve. Do your best to be completely professional, clear about your communication, and polite to those around you. When confronted with a demand for support, focus your energy on doing your work, and, if possible, remain detached from the problem person. Typically this will draw a hostile response, because anyone who does not prop up the problem person is seen as a threat by those drawn into the addicted circle. But holding firm is the only long-term solution. It will also allow you and energize you to continue getting your work done.

The best strategy is to maintain your focus. Be very clear about your work and what you are trying to achieve. Do your best to be completely professional, clear about your communication, and polite to those around you.

If possible, bring the problem situation to the attention of those who can do something about it. It may be wise to document behaviors, particularly if they make it difficult to do your work. The key is to focus on productivity related issues and to do so as unemotionally as possible, since the problem person will undoubtedly try to pump up the emotional volume of the situation once confronted.

In all this beware. Unless the senior management is experienced with this type of situation, their first response will be to pretend it is not happening; these situations consume great amounts of energy, and many managers hold to the "ignore it and it will go away" school. Also, if senior staff or management is involved in propping up the problem person, *you* may very quickly become named as the problem.

Regardless, get outside support. Have someone, or a group, to talk to. A professional counselor is a good idea. An outside support group will help you keep clear about your own issues and provide support if the situation turns hostile.

It is wise in these situations to recognize our own limitations. Yes, we want to help. But people with addictions and personality problems need caring and firm confrontation from people who know what they are doing. We, as co-workers and associates, are rarely trained and experienced in this type of intervention. We need to stand clear and leave the major work of healing to the professionals.

We, as co-workers and associates, are rarely trained and experienced in this type of intervention. We need to stand clear and leave the major work of healing to the professionals.

In this regard, a good employee assistance program (EAP) will have resource people with experience in these matters who can help. Unfortunately, these programs are usually only found in larger organizations. Still, smaller companies will sometimes purchase this assistance, particularly if the identified problem involves a senior staff or management person.

Termination

One of the darkest parts of work is losing it – especially through layoff or firing. And the bad news (as if termination was not bad enough) is that given the changing shape of the North American economy this experience is becoming increasingly common. Most of us will face a permanent layoff at some time in our working lives. Many of us will face it more than once. We all need to learn to accept this, to work through it, and to help others in the same situation.

Almost always, termination is not a nice process. It hurts and always there are emotional loose ends. As already mentioned in Chapter 2, one of the first things to suffer is our sense of identity as workers. To add insult to injury, very often we feel we have been unjustly or unfairly treated, particularly so if we also feel we have been made a scapegoat for larger problems. Leaving may mean saying goodbye to colleagues we have worked with for years, people we have come to know as friends. If the termination was preceded by a period of conflict, these goodbyes can be strained and awkward.

Sometimes there is barely even *time* to say goodbye. Many large institutions have instituted policies that require employees to vacate the premises almost immediately upon notification of termination. Employees are required to hand over their keys and are escorted to the front door, sometimes by security guards. The lack of trust these policies reflect can be particularly hurtful to long-time workers, who have invested years in a job and who genuinely care about the well-being of the institution. (Naming these as destructive practices may be a first step in finding more humane ways to go about this business, which is already destructive enough.)

On the other side of things, closure can *also* be difficult for those who remain behind in the workplace. These people may have differing views on the appropriateness of the termination, and while it might help them to talk about the details, this is not always possible. Depending on the circumstances, there is often the question, "Am I next?" Managers responsible for terminations often go through agonizing self-examination, feel guilty, and themselves become less able to function. Even though termination is sometimes the best thing that can be done for the company and for the person, it has deep and lasting effects on everyone.

For those of us who have lost our work, termination is the start of a long process of grief. We experience all the typical aspects of mourning – denial and anger, bargaining and depression – until we finally come to acceptance of the loss. Then we face the roller coaster of hope and rejection, while we look for new work opportunities. It can be a long and very tough business moving from one job to another.

In making this transition, it is important not to be consumed by anger, or to give way to despair. These are very real emotions that anyone losing a job will go through. But as we move through this phase we must accept the feelings and not give in to seeing them as permanent. Anger and depression are valid, but if they are not balanced by a search for new opportunities and an openness to what can be learned through the experience, these emotions can quickly get the best of us.

While this next piece of wisdom may seem trite or difficult to accept by those who are still angry or who are otherwise still in the emotional throes of adjustment, it is true nonetheless. Being laid off or fired is not always a bad thing. Many workers look upon it as one of the best things that ever happened to them. Being laid off or fired can be a needed and positive release from a destructive job. This does not mean, of course, that these workers felt this relief immediately after losing the work. Usually, they used their downtime to re-evaluate their lives, assess their goals, and set a new direction more in keeping with their core identity and values. It became a positive experience because they *used* it to create a life that is more in keeping with their soul.

Anger and depression are valid, but if they are not balanced by a search for new opportunities and an openness to what can be learned through the experience, these emotions can quickly get the best of us.

Still, I wish I could give some magic advice that would provide an easy way to get through these times, but I do not know of any. I *do* know that attitude makes a tremendous difference. My mantra in such circumstances is "Everything will be all right." Then I reflect on my good health, the good experiences I have had, the things my work has taught me and that I value and want to build upon, and I try to recognize that no matter what I have been through, I am still a valuable and positive person.

I have found that talking to others is extremely valuable. I have talked to friends, neighbors, and loved ones, as often as they have let me and as long as they have been willing to listen – sometimes a little more. I have talked until I have become sick of the story myself. (At times like these, it helps to have a wide circle of friends.) Always, their feedback and support has helped me keep my perspective, has given me positive reinforcement, and has served to lessen the pain. (Their feedback has also provided good leads on new work.)

In short, losing our work is painful and traumatic. Sometimes it can also be transformative and life giving. Either way, our friends can help us through. And someday, we may be called upon to return the favor.

Process Problems

At first glance it may seem strange that I include process problems in a chapter on darkness in the workplace. We usually describe processes as either efficient or inefficient, whereas allusions to "darkness" seem to hint at immoral or unethical deeds.

I have included a brief discussion of processes because when I talk about darkness in the workplace, or the shadow side of work, I am really talking about anything that has a negative effect on the individual, on the work environment, on the end product, on the end user, or on our larger non-working environment. Processes may be "merely inefficient," but when they *are* so, they can have a negative influence on any or all of these things.

On the personal level, inefficient processes drain physical, emotional, and spiritual resources. People suffer from overwork as they waste time, energy, and resources on tasks that could be done more efficiently or effectively. This personal frustration soon sours the working environment as people start to get angry with themselves, with each other, and with the organization.

Inefficiencies in process can also negatively affect the quality of the product and they are often a common complaint of customers. One international volunteer organization I worked for typically took one to two years to process a prospective volunteer's application, although applications could at times be processed in six months. Sometimes the application process was never completed. Often, volunteers would give up and go elsewhere, particularly when they found that rival organizations could complete the same application in a matter of weeks. When customer frustrations grow to significant proportions, they can threaten the very viability of the organization.

Any organization can provide better service and make more effective use of worker time and energy. It just takes some *work*, and a recognition that it is the *process* that is usually the problem, not the *people*. Processes and procedures tend to evolve over time in response to changing environments and problems, almost as if they had a life of their own. Systems and procedures grow, bit by bit, as little pieces get added onto already existing structures, until one day we discover that what used to work two years ago has, in the meantime, grown enormously complex and unwieldy.

Any organization can provide better service and make more effective use of worker time and energy. It just takes some work, *and a recognition that it is the* process *that is usually the problem, not the*

The *work* alluded to above involves reengineering or redesigning the process. Whole books have been written about this subject and I can hardly even touch on the surface of the topic. Suffice it to say that it is helpful, according to reengineering guru Michael Hammer, to outline "inputs" on one page, "outputs" on a second page, and to put a blank sheet of paper in between. Rethink everything between input and output, focusing on what needs to be done in order to ensure that the core outputs, or the primary goals, are achieved.

When reviewing processes, it is important to remember that we feel better when we work well. Each one of us has a very deep need to be productive and wasted effort runs counter to that need.

Another concern about process is the issue of *access* or *participation*. Who has access to the decision-making process? Who gets to participate in the discussion when important decisions are being made?

In the past, it has not been uncommon for government, for example, to institute policies regarding land use or resource management without much consultation with or input from the communities most directly affected by those decisions. Closer to home, it is worth looking at how important decisions get made in our own places of work.

Invariably, whenever this topic is raised, arguments arise over the relative efficiencies of a top-down approach to management and decision making, versus a more consultative or cooperative approach. The issues are complex and I do not want to pretend there is only one correct, or easy, answer.

By naming lack of participation in decision-making processes as something "dark," I simply wish to recognize the negative energies that are created when people are excluded from having input into important decisions that affect their work and their lives. The more dictatorial the work environment, the more workers feel powerless and hopeless. These feelings can quickly lead to a nonproductive apathy and depression, or an actively destructive anger and resentment.

The more dictatorial the work environment, the more workers feel powerless and hopeless.

Good work requires positive energy and attitudes. One way to create those things, I believe, is by actively encouraging as much worker participation in decision-making processes as possible.

Moral Systems

Ethics are a problem, and not because there is not "enough" ethics in the business world, but because we live in a world of conflicting ethics, where deeply held beliefs about right and wrong clash.

I hesitate to raise this issue because of its sheer complexity. Professional ethicists themselves do not agree about the nature or source of the ethical problems we face in the workplace. Yet this is another one of the areas where our work can become very painful for ourselves and for those we work with. While I do not claim to be an expert in this field, I do believe that we need to have a grasp of the basic issues and how we might respond. I believe this is particularly important as our workplaces begin to straddle the globe and we encounter a greater diversity of people and moral and ethical systems.

To give just a little taste of the complexity of these issues, over time and between locations, ethics and morality change. For example, in North America we have learned that "humanocentric" ethics and morality are not adequate. We have learned that it is *not right* to cut down all the trees, leave gaping wounds in the Earth, or to pump poisons into rivers by the ton in order to serve *human* desires. We now believe that these activities are *wrong*. But our ecologically sensitive ethics are something new. We *once* thought that it was our right to do these things, that these were reasonable activities moral and ethical human beings could engage in.

But while we now know that destroying the Earth is *not* moral, we are still deeply divided when it comes to the morality of nuclear war, capital punishment, euthanasia, abortion, or any number of other issues. Genuinely moral and ethical people can stand completely opposed when it comes to these things.

These issues also have a connection to our work. Is it moral to supply parts for weapons manufacture? Is it moral to prescribe drugs knowing they will be used to end a life? Is it moral to operate an abortion clinic? And is it moral to be any part of the long economic chain involved with these – the truckers, cleaners, accountants, or lawyers necessary for their operation as businesses? Is it moral to have your products, even though passed through wholesalers and suppliers, come into these businesses? There are those who answer "yes" and those who answer "no" to each of these questions. What happens if it is our boss who answers "yes" and we who answer "no"?

Then, too, what happens when we take our commonly held North American ethics into other countries? For example, what happens when the deeply held North American belief (backed by North American law) that our families should not prosper at the expense of our business partners meets the deeply held African belief (backed by thousands of years of cultural and economic practice) that family needs precede all other loyalties? Or what about when our requirement of private ownership (the basis of our economic system) meets a Marxist commitment to collective well-being? We are not talking about abstractions; these are realities faced by companies and organizations all over the planet. Value systems – and along with them, morality, ethics, and law – clash on a regular basis.

The results range from amusing to devastating.

So what can we do? I am not sure what the answer is, or even if there is one. As I said, even professional ethicists disagree about these issues.

My personal solution has three steps.

Tolerating diversity is one way I can be open to the richness life has to offer, and it provides an opportunity to learn new ways of thinking and to gain new perspec-

1. Tolerance

I cannot make others believe what I believe, or be-have in ways I believe are moral and ethical. What I *can* do is try to be tolerant of the range of perspectives and practices of other human beings. Diversity is good. It is a sign of life and growth. Tolerating diversity is one way I can be open to the richness life has to offer, and it provides an opportunity to learn new ways of thinking and to gain new perspectives.

In Chapter 3, I described the process of work as beginning with imagination. Imagination springs from, among other things, diversity. Diversity pushes us to see new needs, learn new methods, and experience alternative outcomes. New ideas and new jobs are common outcomes of the experience of diversity.

But sometimes diversity is not comfortable. As I said in Chapter 2, we have a need to see our own face reflected in the world. Diversity can rub up against the edges of our personal comfort zone and leave us wishing that people and processes were more like us. Many organizations and companies recognize and deal with this by offering formal programs that help people to become more comfortable with diversity.

2. Clarity

Sometimes the issues feel closer to home than mere diversity. Sometimes the issues strike us as being blatantly about *right* and *wrong*. To talk of tolerance in these situations is not very helpful. These clashes seem "either-or."

What we can do when faced with these clashes is try to be *clear* about *who we are* and *what we believe*. Rarely are these ethical clashes about good people versus bad people (no matter how much either side may wish to put it in these terms). If possible, we can try to express our ethics in terms comfortable to the other party. Clear communication breaks down barriers and can help create a situation of *compromise*.

But few of us are that capable and articulate. Generally, the most we can say is, "Work with me. Let us walk together, and at some point in the future you may trust me regardless of how different I sound."

Here lies one of work's greatest powers and rewards. In these situations bridges are usually built, not out of understanding and shared language, but out of shared *experience*. As we work together, we learn that constructive experiences can happen for both sides. Because work forces us to join together as human beings to accomplish shared ends, it teaches us that we need each other despite our differences. We can learn to respect each other and compromise in many places, even when we disagree profoundly.

3. Non-violent Resistance

Occasionally, these two strategies are not enough. As we will see, in Chapter 10, there are very different ways of understanding the true nature of the universe, ways of understanding that change the way we see right and wrong. Some ways of understanding the nature of the universe may, under some circumstances, lead to *violence* against other people or the planet. At these points, I believe we are called to non-violent *resistance*.

Resistance means, first of all, refusing to be *complicit*. It means saying, "If that is what it means to be part of this, then I will not participate." Our resistance begins by disconnecting ourselves from the behavior we find immoral, unethical, or illegal.

In the workplace, this may mean quitting your job. This may be all you can do. It may also be enough. Often it is our complicity that allows behaviors we disapprove of to continue. Most people want to do what is right and when we take a stand they will often change their behavior. They may not agree with our stance, but they seek to maintain our good will and relationship. Even if this scenario seems only to postpone further conflict, that postponement may provide the necessary time for education to take place, or for a joint search for a mutually acceptable process or outcome.

> *Resistance means, first of all, refusing to be* complicit...*Our resistance begins by disconnecting ourselves from the behavior we find immoral, unethical, or illegal.*

But sometimes we find ourselves faced with a refusal to listen and no consideration given to changing. Then we may need to take a second step of resistance, which is to say, "I will do my best to ensure that you may not continue." "Whistle-blowing" by turning to the law or the public is one way to do this. *Boycotts* and *public awareness* campaigns can also work to change the behavior of those who will not listen. These strategies can be risky and need to happen with the support of a community.

One of the strengths of *democracy* is that if we can convince a majority that a certain thing is wrong, we can make laws against it. While democracy is a slow and cumbersome process, it works reasonably well.

Is it right to ever resist violently? I personally do not believe that it is right to use violence against others, even when that violence may stop an injustice. Fortunately, this question very rarely needs to be asked in our workplaces, and in those few cases where it might, I recommend a long process of consultation.

Tedium

One of the basic problems we all deal with in our work, at some time, is tedium. Our tasks become wearisome and boring. Our work does not *give* us energy, but rather *drains* our energy. In some cases, this can even bring us into physical danger as our boredom causes us to lose awareness of the risks in our physical environment.

Which tasks we find draining depends very much on who we are. While I may find a particular set of routines tedious, that does not mean that others will find them so. The challenge is to judge our own limits and to find ways of working within them. Personally, I hate filing. But I have learned to co-exist with it in a rather messy relationship. My filing cabinet is half-empty, while files in various states of disarray are stacked on the floor, in shelves on the wall, and in bins under my desk. I do not lose things, but I have had to root through my recycling bin from time to time to find work in progress. When the mess gets bad enough, I sit down with a cup of tea and patiently label and put things away.

It works for me, but it certainly would not for one of my former colleagues, who was of the "keep your desktop clear" school. Every day, at the end of the day, he put everything neatly away.

Filing is mostly an *inconvenience* for me. But tedium can also be *dangerous*. When I worked in a warehouse, the tedium of waiting for another truck to arrive, or for the front desk to send an order to fill from the stacks, left me drowsy. I spent hours rearranging boxes and looking for little bits of dust in an effort to keep awake. I became sloppy in my work. Once, due to my inattention, I accidentally caused an eight-foot stack of 60 lb. boxes to topple. I was not hurt, but the experience shook me up and taught me how serious my inattention could become. What if the stack had come down on me? What if it had been a 16-foot stack? I needed to get out of that job.

How we cope with tedium is largely up to us. Sometimes a little discipline will take care of it. Other times we may need to make major changes. Either way, before we can do anything about it, we must name it.

Destructive By-products & Side Effects of Work

No matter what we do, there are destructive by-products and side effects to our work. Waste, pollution, or product misuse all "shadow" our work. While we can never eliminate these by-products and side effects, we need to make a commitment to respecting our planet and each other. We all bear the responsibility of doing the best we can with the knowledge and methods at our disposal.

We also need to seek ways of doing better. When a new approach comes along, we must be the first to risk trying it.

But reducing or ending destructive practices is not always easy. What happens when there is no better way, or when it exists but implementing it is beyond our capability? At that point, we need to reach out to others in our organization and beyond in a search for assistance. Generally I advise going to people in the company first. If we are to have any hope of implementing a solution, it will only be with the support of others in the organization.

Whether or not we choose to look outside the organization for help depends a lot on the ethos of the management of the company and how sympathetic they are to the concern that has been raised. If they are sympathetic, they will probably institute a search for solutions themselves, and be quite happy to accept them wherever they come from. If they are not sympathetic, the decision to look outside for solutions becomes much more risky. Companies in this situation often find it easier to eliminate the one trying to solve the problem than to face the problem itself.

Recognizing Our Darkness

It is important to recognize our own participation in all of these forms of darkness. Each one of us brings a mixture of good and bad, helpful and unhelpful qualities to our work. Work can do bad things to us (and to the world), but we can also do bad things to our work.

It is not uncommon, for example, to take the turmoil and struggle of our personal lives and project it onto our work and co-workers. I once had a terrible relationship with a co-worker. Things went from bad to worse. Eventually, I began to see my own part in what made our relationship awful. We were out on a call together, and as I glanced at her I caught in her profile a similarity to my mother. Suddenly it hit me that I was projecting onto her some of my feelings toward my mother, with whom I was fighting at the time. That realization helped me to calm down in our relationship and do my part to improve things.

It is not uncommon, for example, to take the turmoil and struggle of our personal lives and project it onto our work and co-workers.

I would like to say that was all it took, but that was not the end of the story. She did not suddenly start treating me well just because I stopped projecting my anger with my mother onto her. Eventually, I discovered that she was doing much the same thing to me. Her husband, with whom she was having a period of marital instability, bore a similarity to me. Unfortunately, we never resolved our difficulties, in part because we were also very different in other ways – we each had a different style of work and a different sense of humor and honor.

The point is that we bring whatever is going on inside of us – from personality issues, to health concerns, to economic fears, to ethnic history – to our work and we experience our work through those things. The darkness we experience can be a darkness of our own making. We can end up remaking our work, our co-workers, and even whole organizations in our own dark image.

I once knew a woman who saw conspiracies piled upon conspiracies. Knowing what I did about the organization, I saw some truth in what she said. But as time passed I noticed a greater discrepancy between what she said and what I observed. Especially as things in the organization changed for the better, and there was no change in the level of conspiracy she saw, I began to see that conspiracy was an important feature of her worldview. As I got to know her better, I found out that she saw conspiracies *everywhere*, not just at work.

While we do not all see conspiracies as this woman did, what was happening as she viewed her workplace was not at all unique. We all tend to have special areas of concern, things that strike us as dark and about which we may become hyper-vigilant. Sometimes in our efforts to guard against those things, we lose our ability to distinguish between genuinely encroaching shadows and what we project.

Ironically, our desire not to see any darkness in the workplace can be just as pervasive and just as distorting. Just as we can mistake the nature of the darkness because of our own shadows, we can miss the darkness completely.

Ironically, our desire *not* to see any darkness in the workplace can be just as pervasive and just as distorting. Just as we can mistake the nature of the darkness because of our own shadows, we can miss the darkness completely. It seems to be one of those perverse truths that we either see things as much darker than they really are, or as much lighter. The latter is particularly true when we have invested much of ourselves in our work. The founders of a company can be the last to see the signs of impending bankruptcy. The administrators of a government agency that has invested 30 million dollars in a social service program that does more harm than good can be the most reluctant to pull the plug. When we have put a lot of ourselves or our resources into something, we want it to turn out well – sometimes to the point that we blind ourselves to the bad.

RESPONDING EFFECTIVELY

Whatever shadows we face in our work, it is important to remember that each of us is different and that the decisions we make about which shadows to challenge, and how to challenge them, are highly individual. We are not called to shine light into every corner of darkness or upon every lurking shadow. We can only do so much, and so we must carefully choose the places and times where we will confront the shadows. Failure to set limits will lead to its own shadowed spiral into despair and emptiness. Our challenge is to find those areas where we can make a real difference.

Of course, all of us will face certain obstacles, whether we seek them out or not. As we learn and grow, life itself will put challenges in front of us. At those times, we must do what we can with the abilities and wisdom we have at that time. Sometimes we will fail and sometimes we will succeed. Always we will grow and become wiser.

We also need to support others who are confronting their own shadows, who are taking on their own challenges. Just because a shadow is not mine to confront does not mean I have no responsibility in relation to it. I must support others by listening and acting when called upon, and by generally encouraging their efforts. This does not mean we need to be at their side all the time. Tasks vary and shared perception is not the same as shared obligation. But an attitude of support will go a long way in empowering others.

Power

In order to respond effectively to the shadows we face, we must first understand the nature of power. Some people believe that power is a negative force. Often they hold this view because they have been hurt by those who have wielded power "over" them, or have seen the damage that this use of power, which is really "abuse," can cause. Other people acknowledge the impossibility of avoiding power dynamics, but believe we should seek equality of power in every relationship. Personally, I do not think that an equal sharing of power is possible in all relationships, but I *do* believe that we can engage in healthy power relationships through the framework of compassionate engagement. Embodying power in this way, we will not wield power "over" others, but rather share power "with" others. By using a "power with" rather than a "power over" approach, we can construct, together, a healthier and safer world for everyone.

In order to make the nature of power dynamics clear, I have developed a four dimensional model of power. How we understand and interact in each dimension affects how we deal with the issues of the moment.

By using a "power with" rather than a "power over" approach, we can construct, together, a healthier and safer world for everyone.

The four types or dimensions of power are personal power, systemic power, discursive power, and spiritual power. Each of these dimensions is present in every relationship and is used by all parties in the relationship to achieve their desired outcomes.

Personal power

Personal power includes all those aspects of power that depend on my personal response. My ability to reward or punish, to possess things I desire or need, or to control my environment are all examples of the personal dimension of power. This is the only dimension of power many people see. While claiming personal power can be a very positive thing, like all aspects of power, it can take on a negative aspect; for example, when *I* make you do something or *you* make me do something (both examples of a destructive "power over" approach).

Personal power only exists when we are engaged in a relationship. If we are not in a relationship, then you have no power in relation to me and I have no power in relation to you. Depending on how much each of us invests in the relationship, we may experience the personal power dynamic as being very equal or very unbalanced. For example, if I believe you can solve all my problems and meet all my needs (a negative of personal power), then you have a lot of power over me. This also means that if I do not grant you power, for example, by refusing to be intimidated by you (a positive claiming of personal power), then you lose your power over me. Likewise, if I refuse to acknowledge your needs (a negative use of personal power), then you lose your power. On the other hand, if our needs and expectations are matched, we have equivalent power or share power equally. This would be an ideal "power with" scenario.

As we approach issues of the soul, our experience of personal power is typically the first thing we try to change in our power relationships. However, this may not always be the best place to start. There are other aspects to power that we need to take into account.

Systemic power

While it is harder to see, systemic power is in many respects far more important. Systemic power is the power built into organizational and social systems. We are all surrounded by systems that embody power: economic systems, legal systems, kinship networks, organizational systems, cultural traditions, and so on. If an organization has rules for promotion and I am part of that organization, then those rules govern my ability to achieve. As long as we conform to those rules, we can do well. Once we depart from those rules, we lose our access to resources, or worse.

Those same organizational rules also establish specific people as powerful by virtue of their *role* within the system. A school principal may be powerful as a person – she may be competent, articulate, and administratively effective – but her real power exists because the school as a system gives her power. Should she be replaced, the next principal would be granted exactly the same power by the system, in relation to the same teachers and students, even if she were less competent, articulate, or administratively effective.

Because many people contribute to them, and because they are the means through which most resources are distributed in our society, these systems are extremely powerful. They have much organizational inertia and will carry those involved with them toward any objective they have. This makes them exceeding dangerous if they are headed in a direction that is ultimately hurtful or destructive. They will grind along for a long time, creating enormous havoc all around them, before they come to a halt. We can see this in the automobile industry's resistance to the implementation of pollution controls, or the tobacco industry's denial of any link between smoking and lung cancer. Eventually, harmful systems will be forced to change direction, but often not until after severe damage to human health or the environment has been done.

As an individual, it is particularly difficult to stop or address misuses of systemic power.

Typically, it is very difficult for an individual to engage with or use systemic power. As an individual, it is particularly difficult to stop or address *misuses* of systemic power. And yet understanding systemic power and working with it is one of the most effective ways of changing society. As well, if we want to compassionately engage with the world, it will primarily be through our participation in systems that we do so. Rarely do we live on our own and even more rarely do we work on our own. Rather, we enact or live out the meaning of our existence from within systems and so we must be sensitive to how they work and to the destiny they hold for those who participate in them.

What this really implies, of course, is that we *can* in fact augment or improve systems through our whole hearted participation. If, for example, a large community of like-minded people work together to compassionately engage a corrupt system, they can indeed bring about positive transformation. We only have to remember the work of Dr. Martin Luther King, Jr. and the Civil Rights Movement to see that this is true. Likewise, if we find systems that are working creatively to build people up, and where we feel personally comfortable, then our compassionate engagement can only make those systems even stronger. Opportunities like these are a true example of soul work, and are something we can all look for and celebrate when they occur.

Discursive power

The third dimension or type of power is found in our signs and symbols, our language and metaphors. It exists in the discourse that takes place between and among us. Every time we communicate, we shape each other's perceptions and behavior through the forms of our language. This is sometimes the most profound power available to us, and sometimes the strongest power active in a situation.

Every time we communicate, we shape each other's perceptions and behavior through the forms of our language.

The power of discourse lies in the way it controls our thinking. When someone describes something, they draw upon all the language they have available to communicate what they perceive. They may use emotionally loaded language, or technically descriptive language, or wildly imaginative language; all to communicate what they think is most important about the object. When we receive the words, we respond to them based on the way they are phrased. This makes our choice of language incredibly important, because whole fields of response can be opened up or shut off, depending the language we use.

Imagine that the CEO of a large company circulates a memo to all of the employees of that company. The memo reads, "The company is entering a very difficult time of transition." If the CEO does not go on to describe the transition and how it will affect the employees, then most of the employees will probably assume that "transition" means job losses. Anxiety will run rampant, people will start updating their resumes or take that job offer they weren't sure about. The transformation of the organization and the effect on the people because of this one line will be huge. And all of this will happen solely on the basis of what people *imagine* the words mean.

I was once called upon to summarize the events of a meeting in a report. It was a very difficult report to write because I saw two alternate ways that accurately (but oppositely) described what I saw and heard. One way to describe the meeting would have been to say that everything was in chaos and that nobody knew what was going on. The other way would to describe the meeting would have been to say that there was a creative ferment within the group and that new ideas were being generated. In the end, I chose the second way to describe the meeting in my report, not because I believed it to be more true, but because I knew it would have a more positive effect on those who read the report – it would be more motivating, more encouraging, and more likely to produce good results in the future. My choice of language to describe the meeting had the potential to shape perceptions of that event for a long time, and to change the subsequent actions of various policy makers as a consequence.

Discursive power is something that everyone uses all the time. Every time someone acts to communicate, they are intervening in the thinking (and therefore in the behavior) of others. Advertisers use discursive power to get us to buy things; associates use it to make us feel better about them; and friends use it to change our perceptions about ourselves. By and large, it works.

The way to respond to discursive power is to be aware of it and its effects, and to work especially at the formation of metaphors. Metaphors are the key to re-imagining what is happening to us and around us. As we develop new metaphors (and this book is loaded with new metaphors, including the title itself), we change our perceptions. We open up new aspects of the world to view and create the possibility of new forms of action. A good metaphor can transform the world forever. Knowing this we can look for new and more soul-oriented ways of describing the world around us. New language has the power to transform the world itself.

Spiritual power

The fourth dimension or type of power is spiritual. There are, as I have been saying, powers at work in the universe and these powers are not neutral, but are themselves oriented toward good and evil. Of these, the *fundamental* powers, the ones oriented in the fabric of existence itself, are those of a caring and creative universe. All of these powers are active in every situation. We can not stand apart from them. They flow through us. They are part of us and we are part of them.

The manager whose story I told at the beginning of this chapter is, I believe, an example of someone who directed negative spiritual forces through his work in order to accomplish positive change. Those forces took their toll on him through alcohol and violence. I believe he could have directed positive spiritual forces in the same way, and come away healthy and whole.

In North America, we have generally neglected, if not outright denied the existence of, spiritual forces. We do not consciously use them for good *or* ill, though our good and ill actions contribute to them. But we can change this situation. We can act in such a way that the good forces are strengthened.

Those who are more skeptical may dismiss this, but I believe that prayer is an effective way to challenge the negative forces and to channel the positive. I do not mean primarily the meditation that opens us up to inner reserves of strength and integrity – although this kind of prayer is effective, too, and necessary. The kind of prayer I am talking about here addresses the source of the universe in lament and hope. It seeks to touch the hidden fabric behind the physical world, a fabric responsive to our touch.

In prayer, we have the opportunity to bring the darkness into the cosmic light, to expose its impact on us, and to call for change in response. As we name and raise the shadows we face into the light of the universe itself, those shadows lose some of their fundamental power. As we work to change and to bring those changes to the cosmic light for blessing, they are enriched and made more powerful.

Shadows belong to the realm of the spirit and it is in the realm of the spirit that they need to be addressed. Obviously, we still need to take them on in the practical world of day-to-day concerns. But if we fail to address them as the spiritual issues they are, I am convinced they will reappear. To put it in slightly different terms, the shadows we face in day-to-day life are *symptoms* of fundamental spiritual problems that need fundamental spiritual solutions. Prayer is not the definitive spiritual solution, but it is a step in the right direction. In petitionary prayer, we teach the universe our needs. As we call for blessing, we obtain the support of the universe and increase the power of our actions.

While we may bring a problem to light, and while we may have a solution in mind, we have no way of knowing how the power behind the universe will respond. At that point, we live in faith. The universe is enfolded in mystery, and with prayer there is not always a visible or logical chain of cause and effect. Sometimes change comes in a day. Sometimes we can only detect it over generations, if at all. Regardless, I know that prayer makes a difference.

Taken together, these four dimensions of power show us that when we approach a seemingly negative situation, we are never powerless. In fact, if we understand the situation properly, we are often very powerful. The question is not what sort of problem or shadow faces us, but how we can use the power available to us in the situation to maximize the positive in the outcome. Sometimes this will mean personal confrontation. Sometimes it will mean changing the rules. Sometimes it will mean changing the language or symbols. And sometimes it will mean acts of prayer. Or, we may need to escape the situation. All of these are possibilities, singly and in combination.

We are all highly capable and once we pursue the soul, we become increasingly powerful in the ways that truly count. We can face any darkness and be compassionately engaged, because the power of the universe flows with us. Our job is simply to do the best we can, one day at a time.

Integrity

The key to all our activities is integrity. Integrity refers to a oneness of purpose, character, and intent, which acts as the backbone for all our activities. If we lack integrity, our actions become shadow-creators, the source of problems for others. If we *have* integrity, our actions create light regardless of their success. When we seek to be of one mind, one will, one action, doing our best to reflect in our lives the heart of the universe, we create light. Our own integrity then calls out to the integrity in others, providing an example and creating community.

Our own integrity then calls out to the integrity in others, providing an example and creating community.

Integrity is the foundation of all effective response to shadows. When I face a crisis situation – an addict in need or a process gone bad – my integrity keeps me pointed in the right direction. My integrity tells me I have a purpose and that purpose is to see good come from the situation. As long as I hang on to that integrity, that purpose, I will have something to come back to as the contingencies of events and the vagaries of circumstance push me this way and that. When an addict pulls me into their world, wanting me to prop them up, my integrity calls me to account and reminds me of another path. When I face a destructive practice, my integrity tells me that I must respond, even though it may well be easier to close my eyes.

As I act with integrity, my integrity grows in strength. It is built up over years, ingrained in *habit*, worn into the patterns of my personality. I learn to see and feel when I am living by it and when I am straying from it. As I struggle to maintain my integrity, each experience teaches me the places where I am vulnerable, and the places I am strong. I learn to seek out the places where I can be strong and to build up the places I am weak.

Finally, at the end of life, integrity is one of the few things that matters. It can be extremely tempting to shift ground, to adopt someone else's view, or to go along with the shadows. Fear of losing our jobs, fear of alienating friends, financial need, and exhaustion can all cause us to look the other way and say, "So what." But while we can betray ourselves in the short term, in the long run we are left wondering what we stood for, and whether there was good in our lives. At the end of the day, we walk away not with friends, possessions, or family, but with what we know about ourselves and about our God.

Faith

In previous chapters, I commented that compassionate engagement and critical openness reflect attributes or aspects of the divine. This is true of struggle as well. Moreover, when we begin to act in a way that names and challenges the shadows and darkness we may face, we embody another fundamental of the universe, and that is *faith*. By faith I mean fundamental trust, trust that the universe will be faithful to us and to its own long-term good. If we commit ourselves to change, we will face resistance, but our commitment is built on our trust that resistance is not the last word; change will come.

> *When we begin to act in a way that names and challenges the shadows and darkness we may face, we embody another fundamental of the universe, and that is* faith.

This is especially important to affirm because the struggle is never-ending and often seems stacked against us. Institutional momentum can seem unstoppable, the discursive control maintained by others frightening; yet we persevere in the struggle. The game is not over yet and our actions can spread out like ripples on a pond, far exceeding themselves. We can trust that the future is still open and that no matter how bad things may look, at any moment the whole balance could shift.

If we look closely at the dance of chance and necessity that is the material fabric of existence, I am convinced that what we see is the outworking of faith. There is randomness because randomness is what makes room not only for decay and coming apart, but also for new life and new opportunities. Yet the balance between those two seems to keep coming up weighted to the side of new life and new opportunities. So we continue, and the cosmic experiment of life remains open to more good, and the universe itself trusts that the good will come to fruition. We are enfolded and carried along in an ultimate, long-term pattern of trust and faithfulness into the future. Faith calls to us to *have* faith, and to struggle from moment to moment with its fulfillment.

9

Order

Home & Work

In the space of a few days, I had separate conversations with an employment professional and a mental health professional. Both explained to me, with the bright light of fresh insight in their eyes, how they finally understood the relationship between work and the rest of life. The employment professional explained how he had learned that each worker's mental health had a profound impact on their ability to function in the workplace. The mental health professional told me how it had finally become obvious to him that the ability of a person to do meaningful work made a real impact on their mental health. I was struck by the genuine joy these two people displayed as a result of their discovery. At the same time, these incidents indicated to me just how far apart our work and the rest of our lives are for most of us.

While it should be obvious that our work and the rest of our lives are inextricably connected, it is a connection that many do not see.

While it should be obvious that our work and the rest of our lives are inextricably connected, it is a connection that many do not see. When we are at home, we are told to "leave our work at work," and when we are at work, we are told to "leave our home at home." But what these experienced professionals had come to see is that we can only do this well once we have understood the fundamental relationship between work and home. We are only able to live when we know how to work and we are only able to work when we know how to live.

HOME & WORK

There is much about our work that changes, but what does not change is the movement we make between home and work and back again. It does not matter if we work outside our "home" or whether we work inside our "home," there is a shift we make at least twice, and sometimes more, each day. How well we manage that movement and what goes on in the midst of it makes all the difference, long after all the other projects and processes have come and gone.

Home is where our work starts and home is where it ends. How we walk in the door at the end of the shift, at the end of the day, or after returning from a trip, is the real measure of who we are. Life partners, children, community, and friends are all deeply concerned with this outcome. This is where the real experience of work comes to rest.

This is easy to see in retrospect, but hard to see (I think particularly for men) before you come to this conclusion. There are those in specific fields who have particular trouble with this. Business leaders and those in the helping professions are especially misled. The work itself seems so important; either the dollar figures are so high, or the outcomes so critical, that any effort seems worth it, regardless of its impact on home and family. As well, we tend to measure our lives by promotions, pay rates, tasks, and job titles. All these things have a profound impact on the way we see ourselves.

The problem is, of course, that the way most of us are remembered after we are dead is not by our job description or total tonnage moved, our sales record or size of caseload managed. We are remembered for the way we have treated our friends and family, and for the contribution we have made to the community outside of our work. The important outcomes of our work are at home and in the community, not in the tasks and responsibilities of the work, no matter how important we think those tasks happen to be.

The important outcomes of our work are at home and in the community, not in the tasks and responsibilities of the work, no matter how important we think those tasks happen to be.

This does not mean, as should be clear by now, that our work is unimportant in relation to our home life. What we do in and through our work is very important. But it must fit with our world at home, and especially it cannot come at the expense of home. The two must fit together. We must find a way to move between the two that allows us to live effectively in both realms, and, ideally, find that each supports the other. It should be that when we leave home for work, we look forward to the transition with both regret and pleasure, and the same should be true on the return journey.

I believe that there is an *order* to this transition, an underlying pattern that, if attended to, helps us to make the transition. This order consists of three cords: *maintenance, beauty,* and *meaning.* Each of these cords is tied at one end in our work and at the other in our home. As we pay attention to these cords, it becomes easier to let go of both home and work, making the transition between them easier and more peaceful.

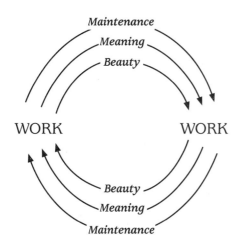

Maintenance

First, work meets our *maintenance* needs; it provides us with the means to sustain our lives. One product of our work is income, which we use to provide food and shelter for ourselves and for our families. These maintenance needs are absolutely essential and have been the key driver of work throughout human history. To provide for food and shelter for their families, most people will work long and hard.

While we may sometimes wish we did other work – perhaps because we have not yet found our soul work – nonetheless, work is how we sustain our lives. Every time we make the transition from home to work, we shift from living the fruits of our work to producing that which allows us to live in the first place. Thus we should face the transition with joy knowing that as we undertake our tasks we are building *our* better world. Every moment of every task represents an accumulation of capital for our on going well-being.

Likewise, at the end of our work, as we make the transition back home, we should carry with us the satisfaction that our labor has produced a future for our family. While we do not directly carry a paycheck home every day, we do carry home the knowledge that we have contributed to the paycheck that is coming. We are constructing our future well-being and that is a genuine and profound *good*.

Beauty

The second thing work brings us is beauty.

Despite a common perception to the contrary, *maintenance* is no longer the dominant reason those of us in the middle class work. While it is *a* reason we work, if we were content with 1960s standards of living, we could cut our time on the job to two-thirds to one-half of our present working hours.

In reality, once we have met our maintenance needs, we keep working in order to cultivate *beauty*.

This may be a hard thought for many of us. When we look at our consumptive culture – at the tremendous waste and pollution it produces – it seems unbelievable that what we are about is the creation of beauty. Yet that is what most of us *really* work for.

I know, for instance, that I could live on a much smaller income than I have. But then I would not be able to afford the house I live in, or ensure that my children have the type of education I want them to have, or even enjoy the glass of wine that accompanies many of my meals. I use my income to create an environment a home, that is aesthetically pleasurable. I invest every spare dime in the improvement of my life and the lives of my family. I also extend that concern outward, through acts of charity. At a certain level, I work for the beauty of the world.

> *We are enriched, and the world around us is enriched, by the investment of our work-accumulated capital in all of these things.*

Think of it this way: Many of us travel the world. Most of us live in beautifully decorated, comfortably warm, well-lit homes. We entertain ourselves lavishly, reading the finest books on whatever subjects interest us; attending concerts and listening to the recorded music of our favorite musicians; going to live theater or watching the latest movies on the big screen or on our home theater systems. We eat delicious and exotic food, much of it delivered to our communities from around the world. We buy beautifully designed cars, SUVs, and recreational vehicles. We dig flower gardens, with rich earth and carefully selected plants. We clothe our children in stylish fashions and ensure that they are clean and well-groomed. We donate to environmental, human rights, health, and relief agencies around the globe. Why? Because all of these are beautiful things to do. We are enriched, and the world around us is enriched, by the investment of our work-accumulated capital in all of these things.

When we depart for work, then, we can (and should) look around at the beauty we have produced, and set forth with the satisfaction that we have done something good. Likewise, when we return, we can (and should) look forward with anticipation to interacting with the beauty we have produced, and to the beauty we will add to the world. Our work makes much beauty possible. This is something we can celebrate every day, as we make the transition between the two major parts of our world.

The more meaningful our work, the more powerfully we look forward to it and the more satisfaction it brings us at the end of the day.

Meaning

The third thing work brings us is meaning. Our work is driven as much by our desire to do something *meaningful for ourselves*, as it is driven by our need for food and shelter, or by our powerful desire for beauty. As I argued in Chapter 2, we gain much of our sense of who we are, and many opportunities to express ourselves productively, through our work. Every day, we fabricate a tiny piece of the future, and with it a tiny bit of our identity. Or to look at it from the opposite direction, when we are done our work, we can look back with the realization that we have fabricated a small piece of our history, a small piece of our identity.

Typically, most people will continue to work long after it is economically meaningful for them to do so, and long after their lives are as beautiful as they can make them, *if* they find meaning in what they do. The more *meaningful* our work, the more powerfully we look forward to it and the more satisfaction it brings us at the end of the day. This meaning does not leave us, when we are at home. If we are proud of the meaning and identity we have forged at work, then the life we live at home will be filled with greater satisfaction and meaning as well.

When we put these three together, we can see that the process of moving from home to work and back again is driven by the need for food and shelter, the desire for beauty, and the quest for meaning. These three things exist deep inside of us both at work and at home, and are the way we connect them to each other. Every day we bring these to life as we enter our work. When we return back home, we use them again to foster our lives.

Following the way of compassionate engagement we endeavor to make this transition as lightly, and in as celebratory a manner, as possible. These are good things, and upon them a healthy world is built. Our work upholds our existence, at all levels.

Many forms of work require that we be available 24 hours a day, and family always requires it. It is a huge and continuous tension.

THREE ASPECTS OF HOME

Having recognized the three cords that tie together home and work, and work and home, we must turn our attention now to the home side. What happens there has as profound an influence on our work life as our work does on our home life. While there are many aspects to home life, there are three that have an especially powerful impact on work. These are family, education, and rest. How we handle these will change forever what happens in our work, for they are the outcomes of maintenance, beauty, and meaning.

Family

In my experience, nothing clashes with work more than family. Both family and work are connected by our deepest identity issues and personal needs. Both demand time and attention. Both can make outrageous demands for loyalty. Many forms of work require that we be available 24 hours a day, and family *always* requires it. It is a huge and continuous tension.

Life would be simpler if we could fix either work or family to an eight-hour-a-day time period. Many men have had that luxury, taking no responsibility for family matters that might come up while they were at work. (Often, they extend that attitude to after-hours as well.) Some men still behave this way, though that pattern is changing as social expectations have changed, and as women have entered the workplace. Today most men – like nearly all women – have to cope with the demands of family as well as those of work.

Many of us cannot leave our work by going home to the family; the work is there with us. As these trends grow and as family responsibilities expand to include aging parents, the tension we experience between work and family is likely to increase.

At the same time, the home has become one of the locations of income-earning work. The "home office" is a standard part of many middle- and upper-class homes. Many of us cannot leave our work by going home to the family; the work is there with us. As these trends grow and as family responsibilities expand to include aging parents, the tension we experience between work and family is likely to increase.

The risk in this tension is that either one can damage the other. Work can destroy family and family can destroy work. Women face the reality that if they choose to have a family, it may mean the derailment of a promising career. Many men give themselves so completely to their jobs that their families disintegrate. Both men and women frequently face the glares of co-workers, children, and spouses as they try to balance competing needs. What do you do when you face a project deadline and your child, spouse, or parent is seriously ill? Children's sports and extracurricular activities often call for one partner or the other to juggle a work schedule. Some people are blessed with flexible working conditions. But the pressure is still spectacular and can lead to major problems at home, or an inability to take on new responsibilities at work. The tension is real, and for most of us unavoidable.

What makes this tension more complex is that work can often be used as an excuse to avoid or as a place to hide from family tensions. (In theory, it should work the other way, too, that we could use family to avoid tensions at work. However, I suspect that any worker who routinely stayed home to avoid the stresses of work would soon – very soon – be out of a job.) If our teenagers are acting up, or if we are feeling pressured by our spouse, it can be very tempting to put in extra hours at work, or to take on an out-of-town project. To the degree that this avoidance "works," it reinforces itself. What may have started as a temporary measure – a short-term safety valve – can quickly become a habit. Many men have built a long pattern of family neglect, justifying their behavior with the claim that they *need* – as family provider – to work so hard.

We need to be flexible – able to move and shift and change the boundaries from time to time, and still maintain the health of both sides.

The consequences can be, and have been, devastating. The family, of course, suffers. The teen does not get the attention he or she needs. Neither does the spouse. Eventually, the marriage may disintegrate. Conversely, the work situation can actually *improve* for the person who avoids their family in this way, since they will sometimes receive a pay increase or promotion in recognition of all their extra work. Success at work often masks problems at home.

Probably the best most of us can ever do to address the competing demands of work and family is to achieve some sort of dynamic balance, where what we "give" here is approximately balanced by what we "take" somewhere else, at some other time. We need to be flexible – able to move and shift and change the boundaries from time to time, and still maintain the health of both sides. Flexibility involves knowing what is *essential*, what is perhaps *not* so essential, and what is merely *peripheral*, and adjusting our actions appropriately.

We may be able to change peripheral things wildly, on the spur of the moment, without any damage. Who makes the kids' lunches today and who calls the babysitter to ask for an extra hour of time might be peripheral issues. More important issues such as deciding who stays home with a sick child or who rearranges their schedule to retrieve the kids from hockey or ballet practice can be changed less easily and usually require some intentional negotiation. And in all likelihood there will be constant negotiation and renegotiation. The issue here is one of relative fairness, as well as the potential threat to job security for the partner who most frequently needs to leave work to attend to family matters.

Unfortunately, in our desire to be good people, it is family that often gets pushed aside. It seems, in most cases, easier to adjust family to work than the other way around. In part, this is because changing the family routine does not show the immediate damage that missing a deadline at work shows. Family members are also usually more accepting than the boss or other colleagues. But the damage still occurs and most of us need to stop every so often and assess where we are with regard to our families.

Family must come first. Home and health call for a revised set of priorities. Those who refuse to act accordingly need to be challenged.

It also needs to be said that far too many employers have still not adjusted their expectations to meet the needs of healthy families and homes. Many bosses gained their position at a time when loyalty to work was expected to exceed loyalty to family, and they are still deeply entrenched in that way of thinking. *They* made sacrifices and they expect everyone else to make them, too. This should no longer be acceptable and calls for *resistance* through confrontation. Family must come first. Home and health call for a revised set of priorities. Those who refuse to act accordingly need to be challenged.

The idea of confronting employers is not as far-fetched as it may first sound. While we may believe that the power of our work rests in our employers or our customers, in fact, it flows in two directions; the power exerted is the power we grant. As we resist, through clear identification of our boundaries and family needs, others will shift and adapt correspondingly; they need us too! Of course, this is not a universal experience, but it is far more common than we usually think. We typically collude in our own exploitation. However, by being clear with others about our needs, they will often open new channels for meeting both sets of needs.

Finally, remember to savor the moments of beauty you generate with your family. Memories provide great encouragement. We will never resolve all the tensions, but we can find relative success and a measure of happiness if we give and take, are willing to settle for less than the ideal, and savor those times when it all works right.

Education

Being a knowledgeable worker means being a perpetual student.

Education is essential for our overall well-being, but it is especially so in the emerging workplace. This time in history is being called the information age, but it might be better called the age of knowledge. The term *information* focuses us on the raw data. But information is only useful when it becomes *knowledge* – data processed by people and given a place or context. Our information age requires "knowledge" and "knowledgeable" workers.

Usually, we process information into knowledge in two steps. The first step is an ongoing intake of information. We must look for new information, new bits and pieces that interest us or that may be useful to us. The second step is education, learning to see how things are connected, and how to relate one thing to another. Being a knowledgeable worker means being a perpetual student.

Study is also a virtue; it is an inherently good activity that makes us into better people. Taking a course exercises our minds in a disciplined way (good #1). As soon as we take a course, we place ourselves within a framework that is not of our design and that requires humility (good #2). We also begin to open ourselves to new aspects of the world around us (good #3). We cannot help but become better people just by undertaking a program of study. I am convinced that everyone should be taking courses, whether through the continuing education department of a local college or technical institute, or from a consulting group downtown, or at a retreat center that offers summer workshops, or from the Internet or a school offering correspondence courses. An increasing number of universities offer full degree programs for working adults. Opportunities for study abound, and we will become better people by making use of them.

If at all possible, some of our learning should be theoretical. While this advice runs counter to much of the Western approach to education, theory is what teaches us how to attend to the patterns that exist at the heart of things. As well, technical knowledge without a good theoretical basis quickly becomes out of date. When we learn theory, we gain a frame of reference large enough to allow us to adjust and to keep up. The social sciences (anthropology, sociology, psychology) all provide theory and insight into society and culture, and along with the liberal arts (philosophy, literature, rhetoric, history, religion) train the student to think critically. When I teach philosophy and religious studies to business students, I always tell them that they have enrolled in the most important courses they will ever take. Few disagree with me by the time the class is done. We need to study things that shake us up and that keep us open to new ideas. Such things change our fundamental perceptions and that is a profound good.

If at all possible, some of our learning should be theoretical. While this advice runs counter to much of the Western approach to education, theory is what teaches us how to attend to the patterns that exist at the heart of things.

Once we have obtained knowledge, we should prepare to give it away. It has long been said that power not used is power lost. This also holds true for knowledge. Knowledge is fleeting and those who do not use it very quickly lose it. This is not because they no longer know things, but because the world has moved on and what was useful knowledge has now become at best interesting trivia. Giving knowledge away is also the way of wisdom for anyone who wishes to lead. It is a gentle and generous way to power. We are all short on knowledge these days, and those who provide it well and generously quickly become important in our lives.

Finally, one of the greatest reasons to pursue education as part of our search for wholeness is because study opens the door to serendipity. Things learned in one place often apply in completely different places. The history of invention is filled with people looking for one thing and finding another. We are non-linear people living in a non-linear world, and so a wandering path is perhaps the surest course. We need to keep exploring if we are to discover the potential embedded in us and in the world around us. The world is full of wonder, and study is the fastest road to finding it.

In my own experience, I have found that my background in church ministry has prepared me for the business world in ways I never expected. In fact, I would rank a Master of Divinity degree on a par with a Master of Business Administration degree in terms of its relevance to the business world – particularly when it comes to working with highly complex situations, motivating people to excel, or being able to understand the social aspects of a problem. In other words, I never set out to become a business person, but the serendipitous possibilities my path has created are at times wonderful to behold. Those same possibilities are open to *everyone* who follows the path of education.

Rest and Recreation

The relationship between rest and recreation and work is a complex one. Usually we think of them as opposites. We work to earn the money that will allow us to do the recreational things we enjoy. We need one for the other. And, we think, we *enjoy* one more than the other.

We tend to think of rest and recreation as the ultimate goal of our working lives. Many of us enjoy travel, holidays, taking part in sports, hobbies and crafts, rest and relaxation. We look forward to retiring with enough financial security to allow us to do these things until we die. But this is the real story for very few of us. It rings true until it actually happens. Just ask someone who has been retired long enough to have moved past the first blush of excitement. Or someone who has suddenly become wealthy. Having spent years in productive labor, we find too much rest and recreation a terrible experience. Someone once defined hell as "getting what you want" and, indeed, the emptiness of recreation as an end in itself drives many to despair. Once we actually get it, the opportunity to spend our lives slouched in front of a TV or perpetually stuck on the golf links becomes a trap.

To find the right balance of recreation and work, we must be attuned to the needs of our bodies, our work, and our communities.

I do not mean to imply that recreation and rest are not important. They are very important. But they are not the point of life.

Most of us are looking for balance. We want movement between production and consumption, between work and rest. We are not happy with either one by itself. We need to find time to rest from our work, to re-create ourselves. At the same time, we need to go back to work to fulfill our urge to be productive participants in the world.

The difficulty lies is finding the right rhythm. We cannot depend on the seasons or the patterns of our work to provide it. To find the right balance of recreation and work, we must be attuned to the needs of our bodies, our work, and our communities. Each of these plays a vital role in signaling the right times for recreation and work.

All work drains us of energy. Our bodies wind down and give out as we work. It can happen quickly or slowly, our exhaustion can be physical or mental. Regardless, our work takes something out of us and so we need to take breaks. This does not mean that all of us will follow or need the same pattern of work and recreation. Each of us must be sensitive to where and when we are wearing out.

The fact that we wear out regardless of the type of work we do also means that we need to attend, in our rest and recreation, to the parts of our lives which may not get the attention they deserve at work. For office workers, that usually means physical fitness. With busy schedules, sedentary jobs, and few obvious physical demands placed on us, we let ourselves become unfit. That means that our recreational activity should incorporate elements of physical exercise. We need to walk, run, or swim on a regular basis. These things become an essential part of self-care, for wellness in all parts of our lives. We cannot be whole if our bodies are not well.

Likewise, if our jobs incorporate physical exercise but little intellectual stimulation, we need to attend to our mental fitness. Like everything else about us, our minds weaken if we do nothing to exercise them. Reading, engaging in intelligent conversation with friends, taking a course, doing the crossword puzzle are all excellent recreational activities that exercise our minds, help us to think more clearly, and build long-term mental health.

Of course, our recreational activities can also compensate in very profound ways for other deficiencies at work. We all have multiple talents, interests, and capabilities; multiple places where we can engage the world in personally fulfilling and transformative ways. For only a few of us does work provide a satisfactory outlet for all of these. Personally, I am drawn in at least three very different directions. One is problem solving. I love to solve deep and complex organizational problems, ideally with a financial component. I also love art and creativity. My third love is for issues of meaning. Now, problem solving tends to be a marketable skill and it is the basis of some of my most satisfying work. But my other interests find little expression "on the job" and so I allow these to bloom in my recreation. I take night and Internet classes in philosophy and theology, and I get out with my camera and take pictures. In this way I achieve a degree of balance in regard to these interests, capabilities, and needs.

Finally, our recreational activities can lead us closer to our "soul work." Even if we feel trapped in work that is not right for us, we are usually able to explore a full range of desires and abilities in our recreational activities. As we play ball or knit a sweater, we engage those parts of ourselves we feel best about. Instinctively, we explore and develop our natural gifts and interests. Coaching the little league baseball team develops a wide range of management and organizational abilities. Knitting requires patience, a good eye for shape and design, a high level of fine motor control, and the ability to follow complex directions. These things tell us about the type of work that has the potential to engage us more fully, and the skills themselves are often easily transferable to the work setting.

Following this model, recreation begins to look more like work than we first imagined. Instead of being the opposite of work, or a means of escape from work, it becomes its own form of work – a disciplined, productive activity that makes us more effective and balanced people. When we think about it, this should not really surprise us. Despite the notion that recreation represents "free time," we tend to *schedule* this "free time" carefully for the long term. Whether we build model aircraft, sew quilts, plant flowers and vegetables, play tennis, or downhill ski, we invest large amounts of time in our leisure activities and we constantly strive to do them better. We *work* at our play, and we need to.

Ideally, we use recreation to create a life rhythm, a harmonious flow or movement that enhances our work and all other aspects of our lives. When we can achieve this harmonious flow, we release energy and creativity into all of our life, and we become more capable at all our tasks. Ultimately, we will move from our work to the other areas of our lives with satisfaction and direction, allowing each its own time and space.

Lastly, rest is, according to Judaism, an insight into the ultimate nature of reality. In resting from our work, we inherently come into the moment of absence that is the doorway into the spiritual. Our work fills us with meaning, beauty, and the things of life. It occupies our time and engages our imaginations. It is capable of filling and fulfilling every nook and aspect of our being, if we will exploit it to its ultimate end. But it is in *rest* that we come to understand that this is not all that we are made for. There is much that exists outside of the material of our existence, no matter how beautiful and meaningful. Rest is the point at which we deliberately shut off that which we have created and allow the possibility of that which is outside of us. In moving into that place through the cessation of work, we enter into a moment of grace. It is not what we *bring* to this moment; it is that at that very moment we are empty. At that point, that which is beyond us rewards us by transcending our energy; we feel its energy through our lack of energy.

...time is part of the sacred. It is the movement from work to rest that allows us to encounter the ultimate.

Through this we are taught that time is part of the sacred. It is the movement from work to rest that allows us to encounter the ultimate. We work and then we rest – one following the other in time – and are brought rhythmically into contact with the foundation of all that is. We act with our energies until they are gone, and then find that there is yet more energy within existence itself. The soul that rests is the soul that finds the source of all energy and the meaning of the work.

The Paradox of Order

When we look at our home and our work as two intrinsically tied-together parts of one whole, we face a paradox. In order to find the *freedom* that belongs to the whole, we must obey the *rules*.

The first part of this paradox is that while home and work are part of one whole, the two really *are* different. *The rules of the workplace are not the rules of home, nor can they be. Yet we must be the same person in both places, or we find ourselves torn in two, and one or both parts are going to suffer*. Something breaks, and we become less than we *can* be, or other than we should be. Somehow, we must bridge the unbridgeable.

I have already suggested part of the answer in Chapter 5, where we looked at how to shape a career that fits who we are. As we pursue a career path that is in keeping with our nature and our values, we find much of the incompatibility between work and the rest of our lives falling away. When our work and our home life both reflect our most important values, they fit together more comfortably.

Yet even when we work in ways that reflect our most important values, plenty of opportunities still exist for home and work to clash. It is not polite, for example, to engage in some work activities outside of work. The psychologist who tries to analyze friends and family is asking for trouble. So, too, the standards we demand in the workplace may not be appropriate after hours. Too much tidy efficiency at home can leave our families feeling trapped.

The rules of the workplace are not the rules of home, nor can they be. Yet we must be the same person in both places, or we find ourselves torn in two, and one or both parts are going to suffer.

Another part of the answer involves finding ways to honor our unity as persons, while at the same time allowing ourselves to live differently in the different areas of our lives. This involves protecting our relationships. Friends and family will rarely tolerate the type of relationships our work demands. Our goal, therefore, should be to ensure that *all* our relationships, whether at home or at work, reflect our fundamental concerns, at the same time as we allow those relationships to reflect the particular needs of either collegiality or friendship or family. Each of us must resolve not to treat either those at work or those at home merely in terms of their use to us (actions which would violate our fundamental concern for human value). At the same time, each of us must respect that our work relationships and our home relationships will be different. We will not necessarily try to make those at work our friends. If friendship develops, that is fine, but we will not try to enforce an inappropriate standard of friendship.

The failure to effectively draw the line between work and home is one of the major reasons we lose our equilibrium. Entrepreneurs, managers, artists, and those in the helping professions are all prone to this failure. When our work is relationship-focused, or calls for all the creativity and enthusiasm we can muster, it becomes very easy to get "caught" in our work, to the point that it distorts the rest of our lives: the businessman requires his children to be on display for the clients he brings home on the weekends; the psychologist psychoanalyzes everything her husband says and does; we lose sleep over ongoing office troubles, or neglect to exercise in the rush of 12-hour workdays. In ways big and small, we hurt ourselves and those around us by failing to draw the required lines around our work.

Of course, our work can suffer, too, if we fail to draw the appropriate lines. We start taking too many personal calls, or lose productivity when we spend our days talking to our colleagues about our personal lives.

Drawing appropriate lines and maintaining a healthy balance in our lives would be much easier if we all realized that we are not super human.

Drawing appropriate lines and maintaining a healthy balance in our lives would be much easier if we all realized that we are not superhuman. We wish we were able to work 18 hours a day, plus have quality family time, plus contribute to the world around us, plus write that novel we have been dreaming of for years... but we have limits. We are each constrained by our abilities, our energies, and our environment. We cannot do all we would like to do. And that is a good thing. For while we strive in vain to do so much, *we miss the possibility found in doing what we can.*

Setting limits is key to liberating ourselves in the midst of life and work. It is much like the virtue of integrity, the oneness that holds us together. Call it the virtue of *clarity*, the virtue of knowing who and where we *are*, and who and where we *are not*. With clarity about these things, we can move back and forth from work to home, and function healthily in both places.

But here is the second part of the paradox. *Though there are some genuine differences between work and the rest of life, and though we need to set some clear limits between the two, our work and the rest of our lives share some real similarities.* To get to this point, though, we may need to change some of our ideas about home.

North American society has enforced a particularly romantic and consumer-oriented picture of home life and recreation. Work, we are told, produces, and the rest of life consumes. But this vision of home life greatly diminishes the value we place on work done in the home, and on the people who do this work. It carries the implication that the work done *outside* the home, and those who do it, are what is really important, since it is *this* work and *these* people who bring the wealth. Raising the kids, cleaning the house, doing the laundry, are all less important since they do not directly contribute to this wealth. In fact, the work done inside the home can even be *resented*, since it *consumes* so much of the wealth that has been created elsewhere.

It is accurate to state that home is a place of rest and of recreation, and that, yes, both of those are consumptive activities. But home is *also* about *family* and *growth*, and about *birth* and *death*. The work we do on those things requires discipline and energy. In and through them, we produce and become better people. Home, in other words, is a workplace – a place where we work on everything that really counts in an ultimate sense.

Once we recognize this, we can be free to take up the tasks of home with more energy. Taking out the garbage becomes just as important as doing the filing, and raising children is even *more* important than strategic planning. Of course we do not always approach *any* of these tasks – either the ones we do at work or the ones we do at home – with delight, but we can begin to approach those we do in the home with the sense of value that we usually reserve for work done outside the home.

Finally, and most importantly, a third paradox: *we need to give up a little on the self in order to keep things together*. We need to be prepared to give up some of our dreams and aspirations, and to learn to live generously, if we plan to actually succeed at our lives. Real life involves compromise, giving way, accepting less than we desire, and sometimes less than we need. That is what it takes to build relationships, to grow as communities, and to experience well-being as people in partnership with the universe.

Giving is also what we must do to find ourselves. When we push along a strictly self-centered and self-directed course, we become fundamentally lost. The key word is "fundamentally." Humans are not fundamentally *rational* and *linear* beings. Nor are we *complete*. Inside, we are frazzled and frayed, mixed up and hopeful, wanting and needing others to provide balance and perspective. Following only our own path, we stray outside the community that gives us perspective and balance. Eventually, we end up lost in a world of our own making, unattached to community, unable to see right and wrong, and confused about what is truly important. It is in the process of working *with* and *for* each other that we grow, learn, and let go of self-involved confusion, until we come close to the heart of ourselves and others. In the struggle to balance our own interests or cast them in a larger framework, we become our true selves.

> *We need to give up a little on the self in order to keep things together.*

I do not say this lightly. Like most of us, I enjoy being able to say, "I did it my way." And yet, in all honesty, I know I have grown most as a person when I have let go of my aspirations and have moved with the opportunities and needs presented to me. It was in situations that often seemed like detours, that I found freedom and room to grow. Ironically, it was often in those times that I also experienced my highest levels of appreciation from others and the greatest personal pride in accomplishment.

There is, I think, an inherent law within the universe. But it is not a law that says, "Do *this* and you will prosper!" Instead, it is a law of paradox: freedom is found in obedience, self-satisfaction is found in generosity, and unity is found in clear boundaries. We must respect the way things *really* are and accept that we cannot change them. We must live within them, obey them, and trust them for the absolutes they are. In return, we will find that we are released into our communities with energy, life, joy, and compassion.

Boundaries exist, but they exist to liberate us. In order to bring all the pieces of work and life together, we must learn where those boundaries are, where the rules run fast, and then place ourselves in harmony with them. If we do this, we will find ourselves released to innovate, to act decisively, and to create the kind of world we believe in. Living within the rules, we will succeed in making a difference.

10

A Lightness of Being

A Spirituality of Work

There is a monastery not far from where I live. Within it, a community of monks devote their lives to the work of study and prayer. It is not the easiest life. Possessions are few, the hours long, and the rewards hard to see. Every year novices come intent on joining the fellowship. Few of them find the work compatible and stay. Those who *do* stay pass out of public life, rarely noticed by any but the families they have left behind. But for them, it is enough. Their work reaches beyond the mundane to the sacred; and the work itself is sacred.

Once you begin the journey to the heart of all things, the journey has a specific destination, and some ways to get there are much better than others.

According to these monks, the picture of work I have painted to this point is like a still-life painting of a pond, where the artist has forgotten to paint the shore. For them, there are boundaries: ultimate boundaries, places where the ripples of our existence and of our work finally hit their limits. They point out that once you begin the journey to the heart of all things, the journey has a specific destination, and some ways to get there are much better than others.

For them, that means work finds its ultimate meaning in the image of Jesus Christ, the source of their community. They know their work to be sacred, because it takes them closer to the One who for them stands with welcoming (and wounded) arms, at the heart of all things. Regardless of the tedium, endurance, or discipline involved, their work gives them joy, because it is work at the boundaries, work where the ripples reach the shore.

Not all of us share their vision of the universe. There are even those who believe there is *no* fixed heart to the universe, but that the journey itself is what is important. Yet regardless of our stance, what these monks point out is true; there is work within the world, the type of work we have looked at to this point, and there is also work that focuses on the meaning of the journey. Two types of work, and we cannot ignore either in our exploration.

The kind of work the monks do, work which focuses on the *meaning* of the journey, is not simple work. Nor is it easy. There is nothing about the ultimate that is either simple or easy. The words that describe this work are mysterious, disciplined, ambiguous, grace-filled, hopeful, compassionate, dark, light, sublime, patient, and empty. These words come from the stories we tell of the way of all things, the images by means of which we understand this universe. They are words that create a task so demanding there are few who can achieve it, except those we call "holy": Jesus, the Buddha, the Prophet. Even then we recognize that the words we use are inadequate to describe where they have gone and what they have done, and that ultimately the words themselves are empty. Following these words, these difficult and ultimately empty words, is the work of the monks. They follow them down the long, hard path to the point of emptiness, and find in them holiness.

At one time, it was enough that there were monks doing this work. The monks would pass their knowledge on to the religious leaders, who would (sometimes) pass it on to the civil leaders, and both would (occasionally) require it of the common people. This is not that time and we can no longer leave this work to the monks.

In our world, where there are no clear answers and where there is no one we completely trust to teach us the "way of all things," each of us must also attempt to make this journey.

We cannot safely ignore this work and simply send our ripples out into the unknown. As we go about our day-to-day work, we change things from what they *are* to what *will be*. Because of this, it is our responsibility to have sense of the ultimate direction of our work – whether it is toward good or toward ill. The work of the monks belongs to all of us; no, it is *required* of all of us.

> *Doing our soul work requires that we do not neglect that which transcends.*

ATTENDING

Though they do not put it in precisely these terms, the work of the monks is "attending." They "attend" to the universe, in its truest form. They listen and care for the most basic structures of reality. Just as eco-activists commit themselves to the work of caring for the physical network of life on the planet, the monks commit themselves to the work of caring for the spiritual network of life on the planet. Just as our physical world needs care and attention, they believe the spiritual world needs care and attention, too.

We forget this far too often, even though we may be able to *feel* the spiritual side of things. But that, they say, is the same as admiring the view of a mountain while ignoring that others are strip-mining it away. Every act by every person either builds up or wears away the spiritual reality within which we live. The monks work hard, day after day, to build this world up. Without the kind of work they do, we would all become mired in the mundane, lose sight of the "Ultimates," begin to lose track of our fundamental stories, and become closed the great mystery that trembles just out of reach.

Doing our soul work requires that we do not neglect that which transcends. If we do not attend, as do the monks, we slowly lose sight of what is good. When we *do* attend, we are strengthened in our understanding and ability to cope with the shadowed side of our work and our world. When we attend to the fundamentals, we become clearer about what it is that we are called to do.

I realize that this belief reflects a particular vision of the universe. But unless you believe that the universe merely operates by the mindless working of the laws of physics, then you will have to face something akin to what I suggest. If we believe that there is something more to life than the details of our lives, then we must attend to that "something more" or risk losing all sight of it.

There are many ways to attend. The monks represent an extreme. Their particular monastery is cloistered away from the world. In their mountaintop retreat, they worship, pray, and teach. Thousands of people come to them to join them in worship, to learn from them what it means to attend. But most come down off the mountain at the end of the day and go back to more mundane ways of attending. For the many who do not choose this mountaintop way, there are other communities of faith, each with its own way of attending. There is no universal way to attend to the great realities.

This means that we must each seek a compatible community with whom we can learn to attend. For some of us, this is easy; we were born and raised as parts of communities on the way. For many of us, this is a conscious choice, as we struggle to find in the complexity of human communities a group with whom we feel compatible and with whom we can journey together. In both cases, we join a gathering, learn from it, and "attend" with them.

But the more important aspect of a community of sacred travelers is that within it, we find companions on the way. It is a question of discussion, modeling, talking, crying, helping, caring, and being cared for, among a group of people drawn together by the need to work with the divine as it finds its shape within our lives. Through the divine, strangers become friends, and with friends burdens become lighter and joys become greater. It is the way of all things.

Rules of "attending"

There are rules to all forms of attending.

The first rule is that of *regularity*. If we do not attend regularly, ideally daily, but at least weekly, we seem to soon forget to attend at all. We all seem to need some time of *regular* quiet, a time we rigorously put aside simply for attending, a time to rest from our works.

The second rule is *silence*, or at least quiet. Attending is best, though not always, done in the context of inner and outer silence. Journeying into nature can help us here, because silence is often difficult to find at the center of our busy lives. Yet even in nature, the final silence is the silence we must make within our buzzing thoughts and this takes discipline and even training.

While there are imageless paths, they tend to be extremely difficult. Scriptures, candles, saints, icons, and mandalas are all useful.

The third rule is *focus*. Words and images help us trace the path to the ultimate. While there are imageless paths, they tend to be extremely difficult. Scriptures, candles, saints, icons, and mandalas are all useful.

The fourth rule is *community*. This is not an easy rule to explain in our individualistic world, but I am tempted to say that unless we attend in the context of a community it is better not to try to attend at all. The sacred is not simple, nor is it always benign. It is easy to get lost, or to mix up self and sacred to destruction. To attend properly usually means seeking the assistance of those who can help us see the difference between our own minds and the ultimate reality to which we seek to attend. Even paths well-trod and defined have pitfalls and we need others to guide us. Finally, working with a community is a constant challenge that forces us to come to terms with ourselves and our desires, and to learn to overcome them.

These four rules are not easy to apply, and that explains one of the reasons we do so little attending. It is difficult, in our fast-paced, individualistic world to set time aside on a regular basis, to find silence amidst the clamor of phones and family, to find a focus that works for us, and to find an appropriately insightful and supportive community.

However, if we do take on the discipline of attending, the rewards are great. Our day-to-day work will take on a new meaning and a new place in our lives. We will have new enthusiasm and energy. We will see more clearly and work more effectively. At the same time, we will understand better the way of all things, and become better people than we were before.

VISION

However, a caution: attending, for the monks and for others who are spiritually mature, involves more than a body of *techniques*. To properly attend requires a vision. For the monks on the mountain, it is the vision of Jesus Christ. In that man, they find the center. He is the focus of their prayer and worship. It is from *him*, not from the techniques, that they gain their motivation and insight. It is *from* him that they gain their strength and *through* him that they deal with the obstacles they face in the work of attending. Once again, as in the beginning of all work, to attend requires a vision.

Where we look for the vision necessary to guide this work is a choice each of us must make as adults. As children, most of us were raised according to some vision of the universe, and of our place and meaning within it. As adults with experience, we can continue to hold our childhood vision or we can choose to live by a different one. We can make something of our lives other than what we were given. Either way, once we have chosen this place, this vision, we must take the next step – that of integrating it with our work and with the rest of our lives. A vision of the ultimate either has a meaningful connection to every detail of our lives, or it is not an ultimate vision. That means that the way we tell the story of how things *really are* has an impact on *everything* – on our work, our family, our sexuality, what we buy, what we do, the words we speak…

An Example: The Biblical Vision

One vision of the universe is found in Jewish and Christian scriptures. While this vision is not universally held, it has profoundly shaped Western culture and has had a tremendous impact on this book. I do not claim this vision to be absolute, or that it should not be open to changing interpretation – it has often, in fact, been reinterpreted by the very people who call it holy. Regardless, it is an extraordinary vision that, as an illuminative example, can help us explore the way ultimate visions and work come together.

This Jewish and Christian vision of the universe begins with a story. It is a story that claims to place the pieces of life in their best order. In keeping with the ways of thinking of those who drafted the story, it is set at the beginning of time.

In this story, God created *everything* in the best way possible. The fundamental nature of reality was "good." Human beings were assigned a role in this new world; they were to be its gardeners, its caretakers, its stewards. But they were so taken with their power that they messed up. They did what they *wanted*, not what was *right*. This had consequences; they ruined the world permanently. Nothing was good, or as good as it had been, any longer. Where once humans *labored* in a lush garden that provided all they needed, now they *toiled* and existed only by the sweat of their brow. Relationships, too, went sour – man exploited woman, brother turned against brother, tribe turned against tribe, every person against the other.

The rest of Jewish and Christian scripture is about how to find goodness once again, despite this fundamentally mixed-up condition. Scripture, synagogue, and church are about how to restore some of that original "goodness." As suits any sacred story, it is highly complex, full of advances and reversals, insight and confusion, hope and despair. And ultimately it has no end.

Through this story we gain a vision for every part of our own lives. Nothing is left untouched, not even work. Through this story we can glimpse the true meaning of work itself, and clues to the type of work that will take us to the heart of all things.

In this story, work itself is honorable. But notice, it is not *only* honorable. In contrast to other stories of the universe, in which work is less than honorable (the ancient Greek, for instance), in this story, work belongs to the inmost heart of things. It belongs to the *way* of all things. Work is what humans are intended to do in the very design of the universe. We do not work because we are forced to; we work because it is what we were created to do.

This also indicates something about holy work. It says that all work takes into itself something of holiness. Whenever we work, we partake of something built into the most central fabric of the universe, and become holier thereby. This is not a vision of a wealthy, holy priesthood. It is not the story of a royal family. It is a vision of ordinary people, doing ordinary work, but who are God's people nonetheless.

That is not all the story tells us. The tone of the story turns because the gardeners, in their garden, harvest something that is not to be harvested, and so bring the garden to an end. In other words, their work leads them to misclassify good and evil, and so to stray permanently from their calling. Just because work is "good" does not mean that all things associated with it are "good."

We could probe further and find more, but this is enough for now. This Jewish and Christian vision of the universe tells those who live by it two very important things about work. First, work is part of an original holiness. To do work is to enter holiness. Second, work can be wrong.

These two concepts extend the meaning of work as we have encountered it to this point. Earlier, we saw that work was one of the ways we transform the stuff of the universe. This creation story adds two insights. First, that this ability to transform is inherent in what it means to be human. We cannot run away from the power of transformation. Instead, we must accept it, welcome it, and live by it. Not only do *we* transform, we must *be transformed*. The second insight is that this power can indeed lead in deeply destructive directions. Not all work is good, and we can make terribly wrong choices, choices from which we and the planet may never recover. The corollary to this is that we can work right. There is a right work, or a right way of working – one that moves us and the universe along its better path.

The marks of this "original" world were peace, plenty, and human beings living in close relationship with each other and with the Earth. Any career that helps to create this type of situation will be more "fitting" than any work that does not.

In other words, the story pushes us to question the means and forms of our work. We *do* need to make decisions about which work is right, because this story indicates that not all work is necessarily so.

These are very practical insights. Earlier in the book we looked at career choices. At that point, we asked, "Which is the right work for us?" *Now* we must ask not only if a career choice is right for us, but also, is it right for the universe? Does it fit this vision of human life as caught between purpose and reality? Clearly, our work, according to this vision, should at least be in keeping with the type of world God created. Our career should have as its goal the maintaining or re-creating of the world God intended. The marks of this "original" world were peace, plenty, and human beings living in close relationship with each other and with the Earth. Any career that helps to create this type of situation will be more "fitting" than any work that does not.

This means that there is now a moral value to some careers and job choices, which is not there for others. This story would logically lead us to place a high value on work that contributes to the care and development of others, or work that manages Earth's resources in a responsible way so that the needs of *all* people and the needs of the environment itself can be met. In other words, this story advocates work that builds our human capacity to love and care for each other, or that heals and restores health to our relationships with each other and with the Earth. Such work would be soul work in its ultimate sense.

I could continue at great length. I have not yet begun to explore how the character of Jesus, the prophet carpenter from Nazareth, orients our issues of home, or our struggles with darkness, or any of the other aspects of work we have touched on. This story, when meditated upon, can further flesh out the meaning of our journey.

This is only a taste of the way one divine story guides us, but you can see how it extends our understanding of work in many directions. Those communities who live by this story will move in slightly different directions than those who do not, or those who do, but who interpret the story differently than I have. Other visions – Marxist, Hindu, or feminist, for example – will extend the meaning of work in other directions. A Marxist would extend the meaning of work through its form of economic relations. The question of *who* is rewarded for *what* work is the new extension, and work that rewards all will be that which is most moral. Hindus will extend the meaning of work through the concept of Karma, seeing the highest morality in complete obedience to an individual's place in life (and the corresponding work). Feminists have extended the meaning of work by highlighting the relationships between the sexes, and moral work for them is that which does not discriminate along lines of gender. Each vision of the foundational order of the universe will extend the understanding of work in a different direction. Some of these visions may be compatible with one another – for example, the Christian and feminist visions – while others may be contradictory. Regardless, no matter how we imagine the shape and meaning of the universe, it will change the way we understand work.

WORKING RESPONSIBLY

This leaves us with a great responsibility. Our knowledge of what we are doing when we work puts on our shoulders the responsibility to make good choices and to do our best to see that the world becomes a better place. Our work changes the world, and this is no small thing. In fact, it cuts to the heart of everything. Those who carry this knowledge are required to live and to work out of it.

Our work is very serious business. It is up to us to create the world we and future generations will want to live in.

Regardless of the specific vision of the universe we may hold, we have been *given* life and we are now responsible for *giving* life. Each of us has been gifted with life itself, and, through life, the opportunity to shape and reshape the world. In our hands lies the power to create or to destroy, to build up or to tear down, to enhance or to detract. To accept the gift of life is to accept the responsibility of *creating,* so that future generations may know life, and know it as a gift.

This means that our work must give life to the world. Responsible work takes the stuff of our existence and shapes it to produce a new world where all creatures can live, grow, reproduce, experiment, and create with greater freedom and better direction than they could before our work. Life after our work should have new potential, new vibrancy, new hope, and new opportunity. We should be able, at the end of our work, to say, it is "good."

This is a call to action that demands the application of the best of our ability, a lifelong commitment to learning, and the development of great discipline. It is, in fact, a responsibility that demands everything we have to give. We are challenged to see in our work a lifelong calling. We are challenged to see in our work the opportunity of a lifetime. Our work is very serious business. It is up to us to create the world we and future generations will want to live in.

If there was only one possible vision of how things should be, or if the universe was susceptible to rational analysis, our task might be easier. Instead, we have to make our own way, as individuals and communities, and this means making decisions which will always be relative in their adequacy. We do not know enough to make perfect decisions. We can only do the best we can in any given situation. We must regularly choose the best option from a limited range of options, a range that is narrower than it should be. As well, even within a limited range of options, we cannot always predict the outcomes of our actions. This is why we must always strive to know more about the outcomes of our work, and to increase our range of options. Our task is difficult because there is never clarity.

The good news is that whenever we strive to do the best we can, to *be* the best we can be, our efforts are multiplied, seemingly by the universe itself, and our good work ripples out in growing waves. Our limited efforts have an impact out of all proportion to our ability. The best we can do is *all* we can do, and it seems to be good enough. If we *strive* for the best, we get closer than at first seems possible.

We must also realize that this responsibility encompasses not only the goal toward which we work, the destination toward which we journey, but also the *way* we journey. There are many ways of traveling and not all of them are consistent with the destination. Our way of moving toward life must itself be lively.

Since our journey is toward life, the journey must be marked by life. We must proceed with joy, celebrating whenever a celebration is appropriate. We must proceed *cooperatively*, so that others may join us. We must proceed *hopefully,* so that no one gives up. And we must proceed *(pro)creatively* so that the path is marked with *new* life. The *way* of our journey lends much to its eventual outcome.

When I set out to climb a mountain, I must take pleasure in the climbing, and celebrate the view along the way. Failure to do so leads to a grimness of spirit that will haunt the path, no matter how accomplished a "climber" I may be. It also leads to isolation. I am unlikely to find very many companions to join me if I proceed only by grim determination. If we wish to climb with companions, we must do so in such a way as to use every step, every handhold, as a new opportunity to enjoy, celebrate, and learn.

Hold Things Lightly

The journey holds one last challenge, however, for those who come this far. This challenge exists because life complicates even the best of plans and processes. Life is inherently unstable, interruptive, eruptive, evocative, and elusive. While we try to set a straight-line course and to ensure that we walk it correctly, life is busy sliding sideways into new forms and shapes. New things, ideas, and events bubble up unbidden. As a result, our journey will be filled with irony and surprise.

The divine always takes hold through the cracks in the concrete. Just when we think we have paved the way to something, or have blocked off a path forever, or have built something that will last forever, we see cracks.

I like to think of it this way: the divine always takes hold through the cracks in the concrete. Just when we think we have paved the way to something, or have blocked off a path forever, or have built something that will last forever, we see cracks. If we look closely at the cracks, we see bugs crawling, plants growing, and life happening. If we wait long enough, the life will overwhelm even the strongest concrete, crumbling it to ruin. That is the universe we live in. That is the way of the divine.

As a consequence, we must *hold things lightly* if we wish to hold them at all. A firm grasp runs counter to life's interruptive potential. Holding things lightly lets the potential in each situation emerge, treats each moment with the respect it is due, and opens us to learn new things. Each workday brings new possibilities for transformation, around us and through us. Sometimes this transformation is serendipitous, sometimes it is accidental, and sometimes it is planned. But always, there is the potential for something new.

For those who journey joyfully, and with companions, holding things lightly is a lesson quickly learned. In the pleasure of the moment, and in the give and take of camaraderie, it is easy to let go of those things which no longer fit. Like children on a beach, we will find so much potential in each new discovery life sends our way that we can drop our old discoveries without loss.

Every moment is shrouded in mystery before it happens, veiled in potential, screened by possibilities. And so we must work hard, the best we can, and be prepared to be surprised. Those who work from their souls are on a never-ending adventure.

Nine Steps for Those Making a Career Change

Searching for our soul work is no easy thing. One of the hopeful things about this process is that the fundamentals of who we are – our capabilities, our potential, and our deep values – do not change that much. Of course we grow and mature, but who we are when we enter the working world is not a lot different from who we are when we leave it.

This appendix builds upon our understanding of ourselves in order to give some guidance for career planning. You may also wish to refer to some of the other resources identified in Appendix 2. Of course, it is always a good idea to connect with a professional who can provide job transition assistance. While expensive, these folk can make a tremendous difference in the quality and effectiveness of your career transition.

Step 1: Determine Your Abilities

There are more than 20,000 career alternatives today. This means that if you want to change careers, you should begin by taking a careful look back at abilities you have demonstrated in the past. You may not necessarily *use* all of those abilities, but you will need to identify them in order to move into any new career.

In order to identify your abilities, do the following exercise. First, you will need several pages of blank paper. At the top of one write, "home." At the top of another write, "present job." On the others, write "recreation," "past jobs," "community," "volunteer," "church," or "hobbies," as appropriate.

Next, take each sheet in turn and list, using single words or short phrases, the tasks you carry out in each area. For example, you might write "organize weekly menu" on the "home" page. On the "present job" page, you might list "organize staff meetings," "stay up-to-date on current software," or "manage a 70-customer sales route." Do this for every page and keep going until you have listed every ability you can think of.

This can be a long process and you should not try to complete it on the first attempt. But eventually you will reach the point where nothing more comes to mind.

These lists contain the things you know you can do, although it is unlikely that they represent the full range of your abilities. As I said earlier, each of us has hundreds of abilities and most of us have untapped abilities we have never had the opportunity to use or to learn. Still, these lists form the foundation, which will to support your intention to change careers.

Now go back to your lists with a highlighter or pen of another color. In some way, identify any ability for which you have been recognized. This "recognition" could be as informal as an offhand comment by a co-worker, or as formal as an award. Regardless, these abilities are those where your level is noteworthy. In your honest self-appraisal, which is a necessary part of finding your soul work, these are your present strong points. While they may not form the basis of your new career, they are places where you stand out and they should be taken very seriously as you make your plans.

Do not be surprised if the abilities you think are most significant don't show up on the "present job" sheet. For many people, our outstanding abilities show up in the other parts of our lives and not on the job. This is, in itself, a good reason to consider changing careers. When we have found our soul work, we tend to find either that we discover new significant abilities, or that we are making better use of our past significant abilities.

At this point you have taken stock of what you have to offer.

Step 2: Determine Your Interests

Now take your list and run through it again with a different agenda. This time you are looking for the things you *enjoy* doing. With another color, or in some other way, identify everything on your lists of abilities that you *like to do*.

The emphasis here is on what you *actually* do or have done that you *enjoy*, because this is a far better indicator of who we are than what we *think* we would enjoy doing, or what we think it is *appropriate* for us to enjoy, or would like others to *believe* we enjoy. I confess that when I drive the company car I always have the radio tuned to a loud rock music station, but when I leave the car I am usually careful to tune it to a classical music station. The *real* me enjoys something quite different than the impression I sometimes try to give. So be honest about what you enjoy. (You can always destroy the list later if it is too incriminating.)

Now that you have highlighted those items on your list that you find most satisfying, the abilities of which you are most proud or where you find the most pleasure, look for any emerging themes, anything that stands out as recurring.

When I look at the list I made, a couple of things stand out which I expected. A lot of what I am proud of involves creating and developing. Another thing that turns up is the prevalence of words, both spoken and written.

Another thing that stands out is that despite my intellectual interest in things spiritual, nothing shows up on my list of practices which would indicate that. Now, either this means that I am not *really* interested in things spiritual or, as I believe is the case, spirituality runs deeply through my interests in ways which are non-traditional (part of why I am writing this book).

As you can see, looking at our interests begins a dialogue with ourselves, helping us to see who we are and where we would like to go. But it is important at this point not to draw too many conclusions. Our interests are important – vitally so – but they are not the heart of the matter. They get us looking in the right direction, but we need to take more steps. Put your interests aside for now. We will come back to them.

Step 3: Determine Your Deep Values

This step takes us heart-ward into the core of our being, into the stuff we live and breathe and of which we are made. This is not an easy step. Apart from those values we share with our fellow human beings, our deep values do not usually declare themselves easily. Sometimes we find things that trouble us deeply. Sometimes we find contradictions between our deep values. Sometimes we do not have enough experience to make clear what our heart values are.

We know that for each of us maintaining our lives is a deep value. This drives us to work. However, there are times when "maintenance" is not good enough and we are willing to put off or sacrifice our well-being for other core values. We need not concern ourselves here with these times, except to note that if there is something we are certain we would sacrifice our lives for, we can list it as a core value.

The real difficulty is discovering those deep values that are unique to us. To know ourselves well is as much a gift as an accomplishment. This knowledge is often born only out of long suffering. Our deep values surface most clearly under great stress. It is when we are pushed by the world around us that we find ourselves saying, "Here I stand." We also start looking inward for resources and strengths we previously never used or were not aware we had. These resources and strengths often show us that our unconscious has been hard at work on important things that have never before made it to the light.

Being fired from my job, a job I loved and at which I thought I was doing good work, was gruesomely painful. It took place over a three-month period and included betrayal by folks whom I had trusted. It is not an uncommon story. What I found amazing in the process, both at the time and in retrospect, was how I continued to do my work during that time. My values were put to the test and by the end I knew things about myself I had not known before. First, I found out how important my family was to me. As with many professional men, I had invested too much of my identity in my job and not enough in my marriage and family. (In some measure that is still true, but I know now which way I will jump if I am forced.) Second, I discovered how much concern I have for personal integrity. As one who has worked with large bureaucracies, I have grown used to bending the rules, even violating them entirely if that is what the job required. And yet, when the pressure is on, I do not hide and I am quite prepared to stand up and say what I have done and why. I treasure the opportunity to be clear and direct, vulnerable with regard to goals and methods. The third thing I found out was that there are things for which I would stake my life. I was prepared to be emotionally destroyed in order to see that good things came of the firing process for those who remained behind. To some degree, I valued their potential more than my own health.

At this point, I know that my deep values include family, the meaning of "everything," community well-being, and walking in faithfulness to my God. Not one of those deep values surfaced easily. I suspect I will find more as I age and as life continues to throw big events at me. The death of my father taught me many things. My marriage has taught me more. But I have been spared many of those things which other people face and which cause their deep values to surface. For example, no war or political catastrophe has driven me from home, causing me to rethink what home really means.

There are many events and situations that push us into the realm of our deep values. For most of us, these are the only way we encounter these values. However, there are others of us who know what counts almost from birth. Some of us are gifted with flashes of insight along the way. Regardless of when or how we learn them, our deep values are the unshakable pillars of our being.

Here is a series of exercises to help you grapple with your deep values.

First, quiet yourself. Now imagine yourself walking through your home. As you enter each room, stop and remember significant experiences you have had there. Try to experience the emotions and feelings that come from being in each room. Think about what *values* might be associated with these feelings. When you have gone through all the rooms in your house, ask yourself if there is anything missing. Are there rooms your house does not have, but that you wish it did? Ask yourself what values might be associated with these "new" rooms.

Here is another visualization experience you can try. Quiet yourself and imagine each deep value dropping into a pool inside you: a dark, deep, cool pool in some inner chasm, the pool of your soul. Some of the value may float at the surface, waiting to be skimmed off, indicating they are not the key to your soul. Some might sink into the water, comfortable, indicating they are part of your soul's home. Others might become the water, indicating that they are critical to your identity.

Now, take your most important deep values and write them on a piece of paper (in a column down the middle). Around them list your interests. Draw strong lines between your interests and the values which they reflect (an interest can reflect more than one value). Draw a box around interests that do not seem to have a great deal of connection to your values (these can be disregarded). Now circle any clusters of interests and values that seem to belong together. If all goes well, you should have one or more clusters that indicate where the most important parts of your life come together. These clusters are the keys to your good work.

Next comes research. Try listing possible occupations that might go with each cluster. This can be a tentative or speculative list. Once you have a few, start talking to people in those occupations. Find out what they do, how they got there, and what they think of their work. Check career resources for other related occupations (these should also list typical skills and training necessary for these fields of work). Volunteer if you can, or work with someone in an area related to one of your clusters. Ask if you can "shadow" someone for a day or a week to find out what their work really looks like. This research will also allow you to list the skills necessary for the work and compare that to the skills you already have. This may indicate that you have the skills you need, or that you need to obtain more. If so, you can begin to do what it takes to obtain those skills, either through schooling or some form of training.

Step 4: Evaluate Your Experience

Much of what we usually consider experience has already been dealt with in Step 1, "Determine Your Abilities." What has been left out of consideration to this point, and what we are looking at here, is *how* and *where* you obtained those abilities. That is your *experience*.

Get out your lists of abilities. These have already been separated into categories that roughly correspond to *where* you obtained them. Now list the job titles, or the names of the day-to-day roles through which you obtained them. Put these titles and names in chronological order. If that is not easy to do because they overlap, then do the following. On the left side of a clean page, put a series of marks, one for every five years of age, spaced an inch or so apart. Then, in the open page to the right of the marks, write each title or name in the place vertically corresponding to when you started. Then draw a line down the page from the title, corresponding to how long the title or name applied. This could be a very short or a very long line. Each subsequent title or name will move to the right of the previous one, allowing room for a clear line to be drawn below without overlap. When you are done, you should have a chronological "map" of your experience.

Now ask yourself, "Are there any patterns here?" For example, many people find that when they change jobs, many other roles in their lives change at the same time. Others find that when something happens that changes their values, it will show up as a series of changes in their jobs and other roles.

Also ask yourself, "Do any of these titles or names reflect my interests and values?" They may or they may not. It *does* happen that who we are and what we genuinely value find little expression in our life, but it can also be a sign that we are not who we think we are, or that there are other issues we need to resolve. Personal issues, family issues, and that whole host of emotional issues each one of us carries around can have a profound impact on why we do what we do.

Where they *do* reflect your interests and values, ask yourself, "How did I move into that job or role?" How you answer this question says a lot about how you do the practical work of finding your soul work. Some of us make careful choices and others of us work by intuition. Still others find it is a combination of both, with perhaps some chance thrown into it. While you do not have to use this method in your current career search, it is important to identify it before proceeding.

Experience is not the most important thing about us – certainly not as important as our abilities, interests, and values – but it can say something to us about who are. As we pursue our soul work, our experience is an important indicator of how far we have come to finding it.

Step 5: Evaluate Your Training

Up to this point, I have not mentioned training. This is not because I think training is unimportant. It is important. But training is a secondary part of finding your next work. The soul gives direction, and then we add the training. And then we retrain. Training must be a lifelong process if we are to cope with the changes occurring in the world around us, but it is a minor part of the quest for our soul work.

Unfortunately, I risk sounding like a lunatic when I say this. I constantly hear references to training as if it were the solution to *every* problem, even spiritual problems. Training, or so it seems, will give us direction, provide us with wealth, build us a place of esteem in the community, provide us with the tools to contribute, solve the deficit, and find us our proper place in life. Not true. Training that is not wise to who we are leads us astray. We need training that works *with* us, providing us with the skills we need, and in keeping with our deep values.

But before I look at how the skills we learn through training can reflect our deep values, it is important that we learn which skills are necessary, regardless. Training in these skills is essential, whether we learn them at home, on the job, or in school. They are as important to us in our culture as a knowledge of edible plants is for a Bushman. There is very little soul work to be found when we are unable to cope effectively with our day-to-day circumstances.

The following list of necessary skills reflects the changes happening in the global economy and in the nature of work itself. The driving forces behind the changes necessitating these skills are computerization, massive information flow, and human global interconnection. There are many books that examine these forces and why they have the training consequences they do, and I only touch upon them here to ensure that while we pursue our soul work, we do not neglect the basics of survival.

At this point, it is clear that all of us need seven sets of skills related to effective work in the contemporary economy. Some of these are easily obtained and most of them are skills we will already have.

Literacy, numeracy, and basic computer familiarity

Basic reading, writing, addition, subtraction, multiplication, and keyboard facility are essentials for most working environments. While it is possible to still find workplaces where these are not necessary, the number is shrinking all the time. Computerization has meant that even the most routine jobs usually require the ability to read and write, to understand numbers and to perform simple calculations, and to enter the information in a computer through a keyboard.

People management skills

In the information age, all jobs are becoming people jobs, where orders are not so much given and received, but relationships developed. The most critical relationships are those with customers and these relationships require tact, good judgment, and a pleasant manner. Team-based management requires these plus excellent delegation, empowerment, and group organization skills.

Communication skills

Being able to communicate information is absolutely essential. This means understanding what information is required and knowing how to present it orally, in writing, or in a presentation. Of increasing importance is the ability to speak publicly. And never neglect your listening skills. Good communication begins with effective listening.

Research skills

Knowing what information is needed, finding out where it is located, and then getting it involves a major set of skills. These skills can be as simple as knowing when to phone a supplier and what to ask, or as complex as collecting a sophisticated set of parameters for a proposal. This used to be the job of middle management, but middle management is disappearing as fast as computers can be dropped onto desktops, into warehouses, and within equipment. Now everyone needs to know how to do some research.

Time and resource management skills

The ability to plan a day and to organize activities in order to achieve goals is not yet essential, but it is becoming routine in much work. Even clerical staff are expected to be "self-starters." Eventually, I suspect, we will all need to be able to assess resources – be they time, money, paper, computer access, trucks, staff, whatever – and to decide how to best apply them to the tasks at hand.

Critical thinking and judgment formation skills

The ability to follow orders was the key to success since the industrial revolution. Doing what you were told was the order of the day. An acquaintance who once worked in lower management in a bank, back in the days before computers, tells of having all of his activities written out for him on a sheet of paper taped to his desktop. He did what was on the list and *only* what was on the list.

Today, in most industries, front line workers are given control of a wide range of tasks. This means that more of us are required to think well about what should happen next. We need to be able to decide what is within and what is outside of our scope (and therefore when to refer to others), which policies apply, and which system will be most effective.

Opportunity awareness and development skills

It is a changing world and so we need to have one eye open looking for the next change to hit our work. Ideally, we learn to anticipate which changes will be necessary and to institute them *before* they are required. At the very least, we need to ensure that our systems maintain flexibility and that we know how to respond to change when it arrives. This applies to both employers and employees.

Graphic design

Graphic design is the eighth item on my list of seven. While I have yet to see this item on anyone else's list, I am adding it to my own. In my experience, if you work in an office or information intensive environment and you do *not* know the basics of page layout, you are in trouble. Clear graphic presentations are so much a part of professional self-presentation that they really do make a difference.

You can pick up the above skills in many different ways and formal education is only one. You can set out to learn them through life activities. You can include them in your on-the-job training. You can sign up for seminars. You can enroll in a Bachelor of Arts degree program. (Here again, I realize that I am bucking an educational trend to technical specialization, but most of these skills are basic to any good Liberal Arts degree.) Another great place to learn many of these skills is in the home. Anyone who can manage a household of working adults and school age children already possesses many of these critical skills. You can also learn these skills as a volunteer. Volunteers are often allowed access to responsibilities and opportunities they would have little chance of being given in a workplace (responsibility and opportunity are the only form of pay many volunteers get). A hospital visitation program teaches tremendous people relations and communication skills. Boy Scout coordinators learn management, resource development, people, and communication skills. There are, in short, many, many ways to acquire the basic survival skills of the contemporary workplace.

Then there are the specific skills you need to do your particular soul work. These skills are as individual as the task ahead of you. The training you need is the training that will allow you access to the positions, resources, and opportunities that will allow you to do that work. This may include training in a specific technical skill set, particular to the work itself. But it can also be much broader than that. For example, if you discover that your soul work involves healing people, then you need training that will allow you to do this. This may include training in any of a variety of medical professions. But you will also need training in skills that allow you to do more than "fix" bodies according to prescription. You need to learn the skills of seeing truth and of listening honestly. You must know what else is happening in the field, what other disciplines might work well with yours.

Finally, there are the skills you need to stay in touch with your soul. These are the disciplines that keep you in touch with your deep values in the midst of the rush and bustle of everyday life. They can include flash prayers, litanies, centering exercises, visualization exercises, meditation, and the practice of silence.

While anyone can learn and practice these disciplines on their own, it is often helpful to work with a spiritual director. These people often work in the context of a religious retreat center. Retreat centers can be found in most cities, large or small, across the country. Even though they are usually run by a particular religious denomination, such as the United, Anglican, or Roman Catholic Church, almost all of them will be open to receiving guests from any Christian tradition. There are also increasing numbers of retreat centers that represent the other great world religions, including Buddhist, Baha'i, and even aboriginal traditions.

Step 6: Find Resources

Despite the myth of our age that we, as individuals, can do everything on our own, in fact we cannot. We will need help to find our soul work. We have work to do, and this work, like all work, requires resources. These resources can include people, books, or other materials. Consider using any or all of the following.

Novels and movies

Fiction has lost its place of grace in our culture. Entertainment is what we call it, but we miss a larger truth when we do so. Any well-written story carries to us intimations of truth. In each character, we find spirits at work – spirits we can learn from.

The easiest way to use a story is as a contrast with our own life. We can replay for ourselves what is happening in the story and try on the various roles. In our agreement or disagreement with what we observe, we will find ourselves revealed and spiritual guidance given. This may not uncover our specific soul work, but it will help reveal our deep values and push us on.

Of all contemporary authors, Andrew Greeley, the Roman Catholic priest and sociologist, seems to me to catch in some of his novels the urban struggle for soul most thoroughly. While I suspect that his books will never become classics, they provoke much thought about the way God finds us in this world. Many science fiction authors push us to consider who we are and who we might become. William Gibson paints particular, disturbing pictures of the future, but his characters are all possessed of an integrity and possibility that says something positive about what we can achieve, regardless of the technology and social forces in which we are caught. Most mysteries play out the drama of redemption through self-sacrifice.

Film, too, can push us along. My personal complaint is that we confuse "glitz" with "deep," and that, regardless, Hollywood has a terrible time grappling with reality, let alone spirituality. Still, there are gems out there, and not all film comes from Hollywood.

Classics and sacred scriptures

A classic is a story that resonates as true over a long period of time. At some level, a classic speaks to us about what is important in life. (When it fails to do so, it loses its status as a classic.) By reading and watching classics, we get caught up in a story that brings us closer to who we are as human beings and to where we should be going. Sacred scriptures are particularly important in this process, whether it is the Bible, the Upanishads, or some other sacred text you read.

Unfortunately, few classics have concerned themselves with work as we understand it today. In part, this is because the economy in which we work is a radically new invention. However, *human beings* have not changed that much, nor have our deep values, so the classics can still be excellent resources.

Self-help books

There are many good self-help books. Libraries and bookstores are full of them. Regardless of where you are on the journey, you are likely to find some assistance. This is one of the few places where people have taken work seriously and have tried to explore what it means for human well-being.

Courses

Most communities offer courses on career-planning basics. If they are any good, they will push past the surface and ask some of the deeper questions. I encourage you to ask at the local college or university counseling department. They may not offer anything, but they should know who does.

By this point, you will have recognized a shortage of material that relates specifically to work and the soul. We are at the cutting edge of a revolution, and with the exception of the self-help section of the bookstore, not many parts of our society have begun to respond adequately.

When to do an MBA (Master of Business Administration)

One of the questions people regularly ask me is, "What about an MBA?" The question itself tells me that this is not the right step for that person. While I believe MBA programs teach many good things (I've taught in them), they are an extremely expensive investment on your part. If your work makes it obvious that your next step requires an MBA, then pursue one. If possible, get your employer to pay for it. (If they are not prepared to help, it tells you that you and they are probably not destined to work together for the long haul.) In every case, build an MBA program around your work, not your work around an MBA. An MBA is by itself no key to a career and can even make you less employable. Follow the work your soul cries out for, and if along the way it tells you to complete an MBA, then by all means do so. But wait till the inner (or outer) voice is certain.

Step 7: Work with Your Community

Talk to others. While we have to make our own decisions, the people around us are the key to effective career transitions. Start by talking with them about the skills you think you have. Talk over your dreams and explore your sense of self. If you are prepared to listen, other folk will help you to reflect on your strengths and your weaknesses. Take their advice seriously, though don't let it determine your decisions. If you feel strongly that they are wrong, take that feeling seriously.

On the practical level, you will always find your new career opportunity by finding receptive people and the best way to find receptive people is by getting to know them. Broaden your circle of friends and acquaintances. Go out of your way to do things for people; find out what you can do for them. Volunteer to assist them in some aspect of their work; it will be the best learning environment for you, leave you feeling positive about what you have done for them, and leave them feeling positive about you. The more people who are out there who appreciate you, your contribution, and your abilities (your good soul), the more people there are who will help you along the way.

Find someone who can work with you as a transition mentor. If you are serious about making this transition count, you are going to need someone to talk to who can help you evaluate prospects, give you advice on strategies, and provide feedback on what is happening. It is too easy to go astray and a transition mentor will help you stay on track. They will tell you when you have done too much, or not enough. They can even help you negotiate an agreement. (Remember, the prospective employer has to sell themselves to you just as much as you have to sell yourself to them – at least if you are going to develop a long-term work relationship.)

One of the better techniques to try is to send around your "unfinished" résumé and ask for feedback: Does it do you justice? Does it present properly for the field in which you are interested? What could you do to improve it? People are often willing to give 15 or 20 minutes to help you improve your résumé (and everyone's résumé can use improvement). In the process, they will often provide excellent tips on who might be hiring, what approach to take, or who to talk to. If you have chosen them correctly, these folk will also be able to give you a better perspective on yourself and your options. Sometimes they will even see that they need you in their own organization.

But avoid the Human Resource department at all costs. In practice, many HR departments function to *keep* people from finding their "right" work. Their job is to ensure that potential employees fit a job description, not to assist companies and future workers to find their soul. If you are referred to them, pleasantly excuse yourself and continue your search.

Step 8: Know in Your Heart

This sounds straightforward, but it is not. On the one hand, I believe that when we have found our soul work we experience a resonance inside us that says we are home. I believe it, because that is what I have felt. On the other hand, each of us is capable of deceiving ourselves profoundly both into feeling what is *not* there, and into *not* feeling what *is* there. I conclude from this that we must know in our heart *and* be affirmed by our community.

If someone came to me and said, "I know this is what I am supposed to do with my life, but everyone around me says I am crazy," I would be suspicious. I would want to know a great deal more before agreeing (or disagreeing). More often I see that when we have genuinely found the time-space for our soul work, those around us accept it. There is both an internal and external inevitability about it. Our inner voice will resonate not only with our tasks, but with outer voices as well.

Still, this does not mean we will *never* hear objections and stories certainly exist of people who have found their soul work and who have rightly affirmed it over the protests of their communities.

When I found my calling, it was with a profound "Ah ha!" and I had tears in my eyes. Others recognized that calling as well and if they had not, and if other circumstances had not combined to reinforce that calling, I would be prepared to think I had been mistaken.

But that has not happened. Instead, my path, regardless of how it has twisted and turned, has reinforced for me the knowledge of what I am to do. I believe we can each achieve this same place, where, in our hearts, we know what our soul work is to be.

Step 9: Get Going

It may not seem to make sense to include a section on getting started in a larger section on the same theme. By now, everything should have added up to a whole range of ideas and plans. All we have to do is start with Step 1 and proceed. However, my reason for including this section is to suggest the opposite. I want to discourage you from proceeding immediately.

Exploring your soul work is a serious business and we are not always ready to proceed. Carry on with your life as it is. You may have other life issues that need to be dealt with first. Also recognize that this task is not for the fainthearted. Finding your soul work can be a very lengthy process, with some difficult passages. If everything in your life is relatively well now, then it may be that you are in the right place at the moment. When the time comes to proceed, you will know it. When we are prepared to make changes, things seem to start to change of their own accord. Then it is often a matter of hanging on tight, as our life takes off on its own.

And remember: as long as you work with honesty and integrity to find your soul work, in some measure you will already be doing it. The journey is as important as the outcome and the path of the soul is *always* open for those who genuinely seek it.

APPENDIX TWO

Resources

Among the many resources used to develop the material for this book, each of the following has been especially valuable.

Prayer
Bloom, Anthony. *Beginning to Pray*. New York: Paulist Press, 1970.
Loder, Ted. *Guerillas of Grace*. Philadelphia: Innisfree, 1984.

Career Transitions
Bolles, Richard. *What Color Is Your Parachute?* Berkeley: Ten Speed Press, 1972, 1975–2004.
Bridges, William. *JobShift*. New York: Perseus Books Group, 1995.
Dent, Harry. *Job Shock*. New York: Diane Books Publishing Company, 1995.

Business & Society
Ellul, Jacques. *The Technological Society*. New York: Vintage, 1967.
Foot, David. *Boom, Bust & Echo 2000*. Toronto: Stoddart Publishers, 1998.
Illich, Ivan. *Gender*. New York: M. Boyars, 1983.
Schumacher, E. F. *Small Is Beautiful: Economics as if People Mattered*. New York: Perennial, 1989.
Senge, Peter. *The Fifth Discipline*. New York: Currency, 1994.
Stewart, Thomas. *Intellectual Capital*. New York: Currency, 1997.

Philosophy, Ethics, & Theology

Bible, The. The Book of Micah and "The Sermon on the Mount" in the Gospel of Matthew, chapters 5–7.

Hauerwas, Stanley and William Willimon. *Resident Aliens*. Nashville: Abingdon, 1989.

Heschel, Abraham Joshua. *The Sabbath*. New York: Farrar, Straus and Giroux, 1975.

Kirby, Gary and Jeffrey Goodpaster. *Thinking*. Upper Saddle River, NJ: Prentice Hall College Div., 1995, 1999.

Nouwen, Henri. *The Wounded Healer*. New York: Image, 1979.

Pope John Paul II, *Laborum Exercens*. The Vatican, 1981.

Wink, Walter. *Engaging the Powers*. Minneapolis, MN: Augsburg Fortress, 1992.

Wolterstorff, Nicholas. *Art in Action*. Grand Rapids: Wm. B. Eerdmans Publishing Co., 1980.

Yoder, John Howard. *The Politics of Jesus*. Grand Rapids: Wm. B. Eerdmans Publishing Co., 1972.